ASTD Trainer's Workshop Series

Presentation Skills
TRAINING

Christee Gabour Atwood

If no CD-ROM is included with this book, please go to www.astd.org/PresentationSkillsTraining to download the handouts and other materials to your hard drive.

ASTD PRESS
Alexandria, Virginia

ASTD Press is an internationally renowned source of insightful and practical infor-mation on workplace learning and performance topics, including training basics, evaluation and return-on-investment (ROI), instructional systems development (ISD), e-learning, leadership, and career development.

Ordering information: Books published by ASTD Press can be purchased by visiting our website at store.astd.org or by calling 800.628.2783 or 703.683.8100.

Library of Congress Control Number: 2007921484

ISBN-10: 1-56286-479-3
ISBN-13: 978-1-56286-479-8

ASTD Press Editorial Staff
Director: Cat Russo
Manager, Acquisitions & Author Relations: Mark Morrow
Editorial Manager: Jacqueline Edlund-Braun
Editorial Assistant: Maureen Soyars
Copyeditor: Christine Cotting
Proofreader: Yvonne Finnegan
Indexer: April Davis
Interior Design and Production: UpperCase Publication Services, Ltd.
Cover Design: Steve Fife and Kristi Sone
Cover Illustration: Images.com

The ASTD Trainer's WorkShop Series

The ASTD Trainer's WorkShop Series is designed to be a practical, hands-on road map to help you quickly develop training in key business areas. Each book in the series offers all the exercises, handouts, assessments, structured experiences, and ready-to-use presentations needed to develop effective training sessions. In addition to easy-to-use icons, each book in the series includes a companion website with PowerPoint presentations and electronic copies of all supporting material featured in the book.

Other books in the Trainer's WorkShop Series:

- *New Supervisor Training*
  John E. Jones and Chris W. Chen

- *Customer Service Training*
  Maxine Kamin

- *New Employee Orientation Training*
  Karen Lawson

- *Leading Change Training*
  Jeffrey Russell and Linda Russell

- *Leadership Training*
  Lou Russell

- *Coaching Training*
  Chris W. Chen

- *Project Management Training*
  Bill Shackelford

- *Innovation Training*
  Ruth Ann Hattori and Joyce Wycoff

- *Sales Training*
  Jim Mikula

- *Communication Skills Training*
  Maureen Orey and Jenni Prisk

- *Strategic Planning Training*
  Jeffrey Russell and Linda Russell

- *Diversity Training*
  Cris Wildermuth, with Susan Gray

- *Teamwork Training*
  Sharon Boller

- *Facilitation Skills Training*
  Donald V. McCain and
  Deborah Davis Tobey

C o n t e n t s

Preface   ix

Chapter 1 INTRODUCTION: HOW TO USE THIS BOOK EFFECTIVELY   **1**

How to Use This Workbook   2
What's on the Website?   4
Icons   4
What to Do Next   5

Chapter 2 KEY CONCEPTS OF PRESENTATIONS   **7**

Overview of Presentation Concepts   8
What to Do Next   11

Chapter 3 ASSESSING YOUR ORGANIZATION'S NEEDS   **13**

Challenges of Assessing Employee Needs   13
Overview of Assessment Procedures   14
Analyzing Your Assessment Results   16
What to Do Next   16

Chapter 4 DESIGNING THE WORKSHOP   **17**

Workshop Goals   17
Establishing a Learning Environment   18
Communicating Your Workshop Goals   19
What to Do Next   20

Chapter 5 FACILITATING THE WORKSHOP   **21**

Workshop Preparations   21
Participant Materials   22
Principles of Effective Facilitation   23
What to Do Next   25

Chapter 6   **EVALUATING THE WORKSHOP**   **27**

    Formal Evaluation Methods   27
    Criteria to be Evaluated   29
    What to Do Next   30

Chapter 7   **ONE-HOUR PROGRAM**   **31**

    Training Objectives   31
    Materials   31
    Using the Website   32
    Workshop Preparation   32
    Sample Agenda   33
    What to Do Next   36

Chapter 8   **HALF-DAY PROGRAM**   **39**

    Training Objectives   39
    Materials   39
    Using the Website   41
    Workshop Preparation   41
    Sample Agenda   31
    What to Do Next   48

Chapter 9   **ONE-DAY PROGRAM**   **53**

    Training Objectives   53
    Materials   53
    Using the Website   55
    Workshop Preparation   55
    Sample Agenda   56
    What to Do Next   69

Chapter 10 **TWO-DAY PROGRAM**   **75**

    Training Objectives   75
    Materials   76
    Using the Website   78
    Workshop Preparation   79
    Sample Agenda   79
    What to Do Next   101

Chapter 11 LEARNING ACTIVITIES 111

Learning Activity 11–1: Introductions 113

Learning Activity 11–2: Red Flags 115

Learning Activity 11–3: Tone Exercise 117

Learning Activity 11–4: Body Language 119

Learning Activity 11–5: Overcoming Nervousness 121

Learning Activity 11–6: Review Game 123

Learning Activity 11–7: Brainstorming 124

Learning Activity 11–8: The S-E-T Formula 126

Learning Activity 11–9: S-E-T Practice Session 128

Learning Activity 11–10: Building Rapport 129

Learning Activity 11–11: Writing Your Presentation 131

Learning Activity 11–12: Delivering Your Presentation 132

Learning Activity 11–13: Visual Aids 134

Learning Activity 11–14: Using Microsoft PowerPoint Software 136

Learning Activity 11–15: Challenging Situations 137

Learning Activity 11–16: Presentation Practice Session 138

Learning Activity 11–17: Speaking Opportunities 140

Learning Activity 11–18: Action Plan 142

Chapter 12 ASSESSMENTS, TOOLS, AND TRAINING INSTRUMENTS 143

Using the Website 144

Assessment 12–1: Self-Assessment 145

Assessment 12–2: Program Evaluation 146

Assessment 12–3: Learning Styles 147

Assessment 12–4: Presenter Evaluation 149

Tool 12–1: Review Game 150

Tool 12–2: Presentation Planning Form 151

Tool 12–3: Pre-Presentation Questionnaire 153

Tool 12–4: Presentation Checklist 155

Tool 12–5: On-site Checklist 156

Tool 12–6: Tips for Delivering Presentations 159

Tool 12–7: Top Tips for Presentation Gestures and Body Language 161

Tool 12–8: Guidelines for Visual Aids 163

Tool 12–9: Flipchart Tips 165

Tool 12–10: Developing Your Sense of Humor 167

Tool 12–11: Icebreaker and Energizer Activities 168

Training Instrument 12–1: Introductions 170

Training Instrument 12–2: Red Flags 171

Training Instrument 12–3: Tone 172

Training Instrument 12–4: Body Language 173

Training Instrument 12–5: Overcoming Nervousness 174

Training Instrument 12–6: Guidelines for Preparing a 175
Presentation Planning Form

Training Instrument 12–7: Brainstorming 177

Training Instrument 12–8: The S-E-T Formula 178

Training Instrument 12–9: S-E-T Practice 179

Training Instrument 12–10: Presentation Action Plan 180

Training Instrument 12–11: Building Rapport 181

Training Instrument 12–12: Microsoft PowerPoint 182
Guidelines

Training Instrument 12–13: Challenging Situations 184

Training Instrument 12–14: Practice Session Planning 186
Form

Training Instrument 12–15: Continued Development 188
Action Plan

Training Instrument 12–16: Practice Session 189

Appendix USING THE WEBSITE **191**

Contents of the Website 191

Computer Requirements 191

Printing from the Website 192

Adapting the PowerPoint Slides 193

Showing the PowerPoint Presentations 194

For Further Reading 197

About the Author 199

Index 201

◆

Throughout history we've seen the monumental changes that presentation skills have produced through individuals like Abraham Lincoln, Winston Churchill, and Martin Luther King Jr. Conversely, we've also witnessed the devastating results when these skills have been possessed by dangerous people like Adolf Hitler, Charles Manson, and Peoples Temple leader Jim Jones of Jonestown, Guyana.

The skills to communicate effectively; to present one's ideas; and to encourage, enlighten, and entertain are some of the most powerful abilities a person can possess. And the amazing thing about these skills is that we all have the tools we need to practice them. We just have to devote the time and effort to develop them.

Some people feel they just don't have the talent to speak proficiently in front of others. But that ability isn't something a person has or doesn't have—it's a muscle that can be developed through exercise and practice. We start by talking to one or two people. We learn about the concepts that make our communication more comfortable and help our audiences understand our ideas. We practice with groups of friends to gain a level of comfort in our presentations. And finally we're ready to share our ideas with larger groups.

That is precisely the format this workshop uses. Participants start by talking with a partner. They move on to informal discussions in small groups. They practice organizing their ideas and preparing their remarks. And by the end of the session they have an opportunity to practice a presentation in front of a group of new friends.

Even those people who are already proficient in presentation skills can benefit from refresher courses. As presenters, we get into habits that may detract from our messages. We lose our enthusiasm. We even unknowingly exhibit negativity that conflicts with the message we're trying to communicate to our audiences. To counter these effects we need to update our presentation skills regularly.

As a facilitator for this workshop, you have a wonderful opportunity to model excellent presentation skills. You do that not by being the best speaker they have ever seen, but by being a speaker who is willing to admit that you're still learning. Take the pressure off yourself by making it clear that everyone in the room is making an effort to improve—and that includes you. Then you'll have set the stage for learning in a nonintimidating, cooperative environment.

I began my practice in presentation skills in my years as a radio and television host, and it was that experience that gave me some of the most important tools I eventually needed to succeed as an executive, corporate trainer, consultant (lovingly aka "BSL: blood-sucking leech"), public relations professional, speaker, stand-up comic, and even a Universal Studios tour guide. I'm thankful to all the audiences who've given me evaluations and suggestions on how to continue improving my skills.

I'd also like to thank some other exceptional people who've helped make this book a reality, including Bob Gabour, my director of web development, Mardi Gras strategist, and tailgating consultant.

I'm also indebted to Christine Cotting, my editor. Her guidance helped this book actually make sense. She was also honest enough to look at passages and say, "Huh?"—thus prompting me to more succinct writing.

Thank you, also, to the folks of ASTD Press, who are the most supportive group I've ever encountered in the publishing world. Cat Russo, Jacki Edlund-Braun, and Kelly Norris made me immediately feel like a part of the ASTD family.

And a huge thank you goes to Mark Morrow, ASTD's manager for acquisitions and author relations, who should write a book on how to build rapport. From the first meeting, I have appreciated him as a mentor and a friend.

Christee Gabour Atwood
November 2007

Introduction: How to Use This Book Effectively

What's in This Chapter?

- Discussion of the benefits of effective presentation skills

- Explanation of how to use this book for best results

- Description of what's in this workbook and on the accompanying website

Consider the following situations:

- a politician gives a speech from a podium in front of thousands of citizens

- a professor stands at the front of a class, explaining scientific theories

- a department store employee explains the benefits of a new product to a customer

- a mother teaches her children how to plant a garden.

All of those situations are very different, yet they all have something in common: They all require presentation skills. And, in these situations, even the most innovative and exciting ideas are often dismissed when the speakers lack those skills.

The presentations we make every day range from impromptu discussions in the hallway to formal speeches behind podiums. They may last 30 seconds or several hours, and may include anything from projectors to shadow puppets. But, if they are to be effective, they must include core concepts of communication.

In this workbook, we'll study those core concepts and how you can help others learn to use them effectively. My goal is to give you a "class in a box" so you can step in and present to your audience anything from a one-hour overview to a two-day workshop. And, by choosing the segments that are most appropriate for your group, you can tailor the workshop to your specific needs.

This book can help your organization's members present themselves effectively not only to others within the company, but to the general public as well.

How to Use This Workbook

Whether you're an experienced facilitator or a novice instructor, you'll find that this workbook is a useful resource for developing and facilitating workshops on presentation skills. Using your own understanding of presentation skills and applying it with the format and tools in this workbook, you'll be able to customize the programs to meet the specific needs of your audiences.

The training materials in this book and on the accompanying website include the following:

- Tools and strategies for assessing presentation skills and needs.

- Guidelines for designing your presentation skills workshops.

- Materials and instructions for facilitating your training sessions.

- Strategies and tools for evaluating the learning.

- Training workshop formats and agendas that incorporate a range of training activities. The agendas can be used "as is" or modified to suit your organization's needs and your facilitation style.

- Learning activities, tools, and assessments designed to support the workshops.

- Microsoft PowerPoint presentations to accompany each workshop format. You'll find thumbnails of the slides at the ends of the chapters in which they are used. The website also contains black-and-white versions of the slides that can be printed three-to-a-page and used as class handouts.

All of the assessments, instruments, and tools can be found on the website. Prepare these in advance by copying them on hole-punched paper. Then insert them into three-ring binders for your attendees.

Here are some suggestions for using this book effectively:

- **Skim the book.** Quickly read through the entire table of contents of this workbook. Study the "What's in This Chapter" lists. Get an overall sense of the layout and structure of the information that's included.

- **Be sure you understand the mechanics of effective presentation skills.** Spend some time studying the concepts of effective presentations by reviewing chapter 2 and by consulting some of the resources listed in the "For Further Reading" section at the end of this workbook. Take advantage of opportunities to observe presentations and the skills their presenters use—there are hundreds of them available to you every day on television. There's some easy research for you! Analyze presenters on TV to determine what actions distract from their message and which ones add impact. Watch videos of your favorite speakers and list their practices that you like. You'll be able to start developing your own list of examples to use in the workshops.

- **Assess the needs for presentation skills in your organization.** Take the time to consider the benefits of effective presentation skills and how they could help your organization. For example, imagine how much time could be saved by the concise delivery of progress reports during meetings. Using information from chapter 3, consider the presentation skill levels that currently exist and decide where there is the greatest need for improved performance. Then use the ideas in chapter 4 to design a workshop specifically focused on that need.

- **Review the methods for presenting a high-impact program.** Chapter 5 outlines ideas for making your program most successful. You'll learn techniques for helping learners become more comfortable as they deliver continually longer presentations during the course of the workshop. You'll incorporate the core concepts that you're sharing with learners so that you are setting the example for them—modeling the presentation behaviors you want them to develop.

- **Study the sample program agendas.** By reviewing the agendas for the one-hour, half-day, one-day, and two-day formats, you can decide which format will address and satisfy your group's specific needs. Go through all the agendas, even if you don't plan to present one or more of the formats, because you may discover an exercise in one agenda that isn't included in the format you plan to use but that would be a great benefit to your specific participants. Simply replace an exercise in the agenda you're using with one from the other programs. The time listings on each activity will help you make replacements and adjust the schedule to fit your desired workshop length.

◆ **Design** *your* **training program.** Because this workbook includes everything you need for a workshop, you can use your time to make the program your own instead of spending that time creating agendas and devising exercises. Mold it and incorporate your own personality to make the presentation suit your style. When the program fits you, you'll get more pleasure from presenting it and you'll serve as an excellent—and natural—example for your learners.

What's on the Website?

All of the assessments, tools, training instruments, and PowerPoint slides used in this workbook are included on the accompanying website. Follow the instructions in the appendix, "Using the Website," at the back of the workbook Website.

Icons

For easy reference and to help you quickly locate specific materials and tools for training design and instructions, icons are included in the margins throughout this workbook. Here are the icons and what they represent:

Assessment: Appears when an agenda or learning activity includes an assessment.

Website: Indicates materials included on the website accompanying this workbook.

Discussion Question: Points out questions to use in exploring significant aspects of the training and debriefing an activity.

Clock: Indicates suggested timeframes for an activity.

Key Point: Alerts you to pivotal concepts that you should emphasize to the participants or that are particularly salient for you as the facilitator.

Learning Activity: Indicates a structured exercise for use in a training session.

PowerPoint Slide: Indicates PowerPoint presentations and individual slides.

Tool: Identifies an item offering information that participants will find useful in the training session and on the job.

Training Instrument: Indicates interactive training materials for participant use.

What to Do Next: Denotes recommendations for what to do after completing a particular section of the workbook.

What to Do Next

- ◆ Study the contents of the workbook to familiarize yourself with the material it offers.

- ◆ Complete the assessments in the workbook to rate your own presentation skills and your areas for development.

- ◆ Review the contents of the website and open some of the items so you understand how the materials are organized and accessed.

- ◆ Prepare yourself by increasing your awareness of the presentation styles around you.

◆◆◆

The next chapter identifies the basics required to facilitate a presentation skills workshop most effectively. You'll be introduced to some of the terminology, concepts, and steps to creating a high-impact workshop that will help your attendees not only learn the needed skills, but also enjoy the experience.

◆

Key Concepts of Presentations

- Discussion of the impact of presentation skills on the workplace

- Explanation of basic presentation concepts

- Section-by-section overview of comprehensive presentation skills training

We are constantly competing for the attention of our audiences. Recent studies have noted that, at any given moment, only about 20 percent of those in an audience are actively listening to what's being said.

Attention spans are getting shorter and more fragmented. If you doubt this, turn on a news network and notice what you see: Not only is there a split screen with faces in at least two different locations, but also you have text scrolling across the bottom, the channel name in a corner, and usually some other breaking news, weather update, or promo for a later program somewhere on the screen. With that much sensory stimulation in their "relaxation" time, our audiences can hardly find it easy to concentrate on a lone presenter standing at the front of a room.

This is why it's no longer effective simply to *lecture* our audiences and expect they'll get the message. Effective presentations now must address more than just one learning style to appeal to learners whether they are visual, auditory, or kinesthetic (hands-on). They have to include valuable information, of course, but they also need to incorporate a sampling of entertainment and some collaboration with the listener/learner.

The key concepts I'll address in this workbook are of real-world value for your workshop participants, and they're excellent reminders to you as a presenter. What follows is an overview of the key aspects of presentation that are covered in the various workshop activities.

Overview of Presentation Concepts

This workbook offers four workshop agendas so you can choose one that suits your needs and scheduling requirements. The two-day workshop is an in-depth presentation course, offering all of the concepts that are relevant to the topic. The other formats are condensed to cover the most vital topics with shorter practice times. Based on the needs of your organization, you also can offer various combinations of the exercises from the two-day workshop in shorter sessions.

The two-day workshop focuses on the two main elements of a presentation: the *content* and the *delivery*.

The first segment of the workshop evaluates your learners to see what types of presenters they are when you begin the workshop. You'll probably find you have an array—from the avoiders and resisters to the reluctant and even the enthusiastic. With active participation in your workshop and careful attention to the follow-up action plan, it's possible to see even the avoiders move toward the other end of the presenter comfort spectrum. By starting with minor presentations, such as introductions, moving into small-group and then full-group presentations, and finally following up with specific development plans, your learners will benefit from the gradual conditioning that creates comfortable presenters.

The basics of presentations are addressed in the next section of the workshop. These basics include the four types of presentations—informational, instructional, persuasive, and inspirational. The text also reinforces the simple ABCs of presentations: accurate, brief, and clear.

The workshop segment on messages dissects the three main parts of the messages we send—words, tone, and body language—and presents exercises to draw attention to the way each of those elements affects how a presentation is accepted by the audience. Because this information deals with basic communication concepts, it's useful even for attendees who never step in front of an audience of more than one person. Many mixed messages in today's workplace result from inconsistencies in tone, body language, and words. For example, the manager who leans back and acts distracted may actually give the mistaken impression that the message he's communicating is not important. This section helps learners recognize and adjust the various messages they send.

The section on nervousness addresses the stress of presenting and enables the participants to practice their presentation and communication skills in a small-group setting as they brainstorm ways to overcome their fears.

The focus of the course then turns to the design of presentations, using the formula Get Ready, Get SET, Go. *Get Ready* stands for the planning stage of the presentation. *Get SET* uses the "SET Formula"—short answer, evidence, and transition—to structure short talks and each segment of longer presentations. This is a real-world formula that works well for impromptu speaking and question-and-answer (Q&A) sessions because it reminds learners to conserve their words. If this formula shortens just one of the meetings you attend each week, it's done its job.

In the workshop's next segment, learners are introduced to the presentation planning form. This reusable form is a tool they can use whenever they have to create presentations. It walks the users through an analysis of their purpose in speaking, the likely audience, and the main points to be conveyed. It also helps participants see how the rules of brainstorming can be used to create a presentation.

Participants then practice impromptu speaking and learn about the importance of the "elevator speech." This speech preparation is another tool to teach speakers to condense the message to its most vital information so it can be delivered in the length of time it takes to complete an average elevator ride.

The workshop segment concerning rapport building is useful in everyday interpersonal relationships as well as in front of an audience. We've seen how some speakers connect strongly with their listeners. They accomplish it with body language, by mirroring and matching tone and pace of speech, and by observing their listeners' reactions. In a lighthearted exercise, participants will be invited to find things they have in common with a group in only three minutes. The exercise helps them realize that developing rapport is not something that takes decades; it just takes a willingness to communicate.

Next, participants will go through each of the stages of preparation for a presentation, from the design and writing to the checklists for on-site arrangements. They'll experience the step-by-step process of preparation for a formal presentation. They'll discuss the impact of gestures and receive a tool that gives additional guidelines for the effective use of gestures and body language in front of an audience.

The next workshop section lets learners step back and consider how they react as audience members. To do that, they'll complete an assessment to identify what type of learners they are—what style of learning is most natural for them. Those learning styles—visual, auditory, and kinesthetic—then will be analyzed to see how they can be addressed through the use of proper visual aids. In this section, the participants will work in groups, with each group preparing a presentation on the benefits of one of the visual aids. The other groups will debate the findings. In this way, all attendees get a chance to see a debate session. And, with proper facilitation, they'll get the added lesson that conflict is not always a negative experience. Instead, it can be a learning experience for all parties involved.

Flipcharts and PowerPoint slides, visual aids that are most "abused" by presenters, have their own segments in the workshop. Participants will learn to use these tools effectively and will go through a learning activity to identify bad decisions in design on a PowerPoint slide.

An area that arouses fear for many presenters is the problem audience member. The difficulty of managing a disruptive listener—what is diplomatically called a "challenging situation" in the workshop—is addressed in a brainstorming session that suggests ways to handle some of the most common (and a few very unusual) negative behaviors of audience members.

Humor is a wonderful addition to any presentation, but its misuse can cause damage to the presenter's credibility and reputation. Good humor is used to diffuse frustration, reduce anxiety, get a point across in a gentle manner, add a touch of levity, and sometimes just to wake up an after-lunch audience. As long as humor isn't hurtful or directed at anyone but ourselves, it's a positive component of presentations. The humor section of the workshop uses a few fun exercises to help participants "grow their funny bones."

Your learners will study the best ways to prepare for Q&A sessions. To counter the jolt of an unexpected Q&A following a presentation, the workshop covers the concept of creating a second closing to a presentation. Having a standby closing waiting in the wings lets the presenter finish the surprise Q&A on a dynamic note.

All of the preparation in the workshop leads to a five-minute presentation by each participant, followed by a self-evaluation and a peer review.

The workshop closes with a tool to help attendees incorporate activities and exercises into their meetings and presentations, and with the development of an action plan to support the transfer of this new knowledge into their everyday lives.

For use as a follow-up, each of your learners will fill out an action plan that another participant will mail in 30 days. Receiving this plan a month after the workshop offers a gentle reminder to use the skills they worked on during the workshop.

What to Do Next

- ◆ Review the agenda of the two-day workshop to see which activities target the needs of your group.

- ◆ Determine the length of the workshop you'll offer.

- ◆ Tailor the content of the workshop to suit your organization's and participants' needs.

- ◆ Make room and equipment reservations.

◆ ◆ ◆

If you find you need help determining the needs of your group, go to the next chapter where we'll look more closely at the process of assessing your organization's needs and at the various instruments that can help you in that task.

Chapter 3

Assessing Your Organization's Needs

- Discussion of employee needs assessments

- Overview of assessment procedures

- Instructions for analyzing assessment results

Determining the need for presentation skills training is not as difficult as many of the decisions you might make. Just about every organization can benefit from some form of presentation skills training. This training can help in recurring situations, such as the presentation of information to customers, facilitation of staff meetings, training sessions on new processes, recruitment opportunities, and coaching sessions. So your goal is not necessarily determining if your organization would benefit from presentation skills training. It will. Instead, you'll want to focus on determining what facets of presentation skills training will be most useful.

Challenges of Assessing Employee Needs

One of the biggest challenges in assessing employee needs is determining the difference between perceived needs and actual needs. Perceived needs are those reactive demands that can arise when there are problems, when management changes, or even when a new business buzzword appears on the scene. What trainers want to address are actual needs. These are the real issues that can be improved through education and development opportunities. For example, if the public cannot perform a company's new process correctly, it could appear that the organization needs to train its employees in presentation skills so they can explain the process more effectively. However, the problem actually may be that the problem is the process itself—not the communication of it.

A training department faces other challenges when there's a problem employee who's not being managed effectively and so is assessed as "in need of training," or when "vacationers" use attending a workshop as just an opportunity to get out of their cubicles.

All of these challenges can arise for a trainer trying to meet the needs of an organization. The good news is that taking the time to assess your organization can reveal actual needs and establish a basis for prioritizing your training efforts to satisfy those needs.

Overview of Assessment Procedures

The basic tools for assessing your organization's needs include records, testing, observation, interviews and surveys, and requests. The most effective needs assessment includes elements of all of those indicators.

RECORDS AND TESTING

Records and testing—including individual development plans and competency listings for positions in your organization, together with employee performance reviews based on those competencies—can help you determine the gaps in communication skills that could be addressed by training.

OBSERVATION

Observation may be one of your best means of discovering a need for presentation skills training. Because it's a very public skill, you'll get the chance to observe employees' competency in speaking at every meeting, training session, and sales presentation you attend. Watch for the signs of audience confusion, fatigue, or disinterest. Observe speakers for vocal clarity, gestures, distracting habits, organization of content, and response to audience cues. You'll be able to note the specific skills that are lacking, and knowing what's needed will help you select specific segments of the workshop to include in your training sessions.

After observing a company presentation, ask yourself the following questions about the presentation itself and about the presenter.

Presentation questions

- ◆ Did the presentation have a clear opening, relevant main points, and an effective closing?

- ◆ Can I state the purpose of the presentation in a single sentence?

- ◆ Did the presentation have the desired impression on the audience?

- ◆ Was the length of the presentation appropriate?

- ◆ Do I feel the audience will take whatever action the presenter recommended?

Presenter questions

- ◆ Was the presenter clear and easy to understand?

- ◆ Did the presenter use visual aids to support the topic?

- ◆ Did the presenter exhibit enthusiasm?

- ◆ Did the presenter seem comfortable?

- ◆ Did the presenter explain or read his or her slides to the audience?

- ◆ How did the presenter handle questions from the audience?

- ◆ Was the audience engaged in the conversation?

INTERVIEWS AND SURVEYS

Interviews and surveys of employees and supervisors can help you discover where a lack of presentation skills might be impeding some people's advancement in the organization. It's essential that any survey you conduct be confidential and free from bias so that you can get open, honest responses. Many survey formats are available, ranging from basic to comprehensive. Your best choice is the simplest survey that meets your needs. If the survey is too involved or time-consuming, your response rate will be low and you won't get a representative sample.

TRAINING REQUESTS

Requests submitted by employees or managers are expressions of personal perceptions. Although they're the assessment method on which trainers are most likely to act, a request is often the least reliable indicator of real need. It's best to do additional research on any training request by interview and assessment to determine if the requested topic is the real area of need or if it's a symptom of a bigger challenge that needs to be addressed.

Analyzing Your Assessment Results

To identify where the actual training needs are greatest, your best plan includes balancing input from all of those assessment sources. In that way you can determine if the need justifies a workshop immediately or at some future time. Then you can make an informed decision on what training and development activities are truly needed.

By studying the results of your observations and the surveys and interviews completed, you'll also have a better understanding of what specific presentation skills are lacking. Then you can customize your class by addressing very specific areas with shorter-format workshops from this workbook—for example, mini-sessions concentrating on facilitation skills, impromptu speaking, or project update reporting procedures. These assessments also will help you if you have minimal time available for training. By finding those topics that recur most frequently in your surveys, you'll be able to determine the organization's most pressing needs and narrow your training to address those needs.

What to Do Next

- ◆   Review any reports, requests, surveys, interviews, or observation records that address training needs.

- ◆   Compile and analyze the results to determine organizational or individual gaps in presentation skills.

- ◆   Begin the communication process to identify interest in the workshop among members of the organization.

◆◆◆

In chapter 4, you'll look at ways you can create customized workshops from the materials in this workbook. Doing so will allow you to focus a program on targeted presentation challenges that meet both the immediate and long-term needs of your organization.

C h a p t e r   4

Designing the Workshop

What's in This Chapter?

- Instructions for defining your workshop goals
- Guidelines for preparing the learning environment
- Methods for communicating your workshop goals to the organization

During the process of designing the workshop is when you have the opportunity to make it unique to your organization and to suit it to your particular training style. This is when your creative side gets to play. You'll be able to choose and adapt the exercises to best suit your organization. You'll consider what classroom setting will be most effective, and you'll determine the tone of your communications about the workshop.

Workshop Goals

Review the results of your organizational assessments and interviews to identify the workshop format and topics that are appropriate for your employees' needs.

You'll use this information to determine goals or objectives for your workshop. To determine workshop goals, list the actions that participants will be able to do after successfully completing this workshop.

Perhaps your company is made up of natural public speakers who only need basic information on how to plan and write their presentations. In that case, you'll choose the segments that show how to use the presentation planning form, and your goal will be for those individuals to be able to use that form to create effective presentations.

If your group is large and composed of people who don't like to speak, you're probably going to want to use the two-day format to gradually raise each person's comfort level with public speaking. Your goals will include having participants demonstrate an increased level of confidence in their speaking skills and be able to organize presentations and use various audiovisual aids.

When you've identified the specific needs of your organization, take the time to map out these goals and communicate them clearly when you begin to promote the workshop.

Establishing a Learning Environment

Creating the right environment for a workshop is a vital step to a successful event. Here are some basic concepts that you'll want to keep in mind.

 A workshop is an interactive session and includes writing and small-group breakouts. The best seating arrangement will be a chevron shape—basically, an angled classroom-style arrangement with tables forming a V. Learners will use the tables for note taking, and the angled arrangement lets participants see each other and interact. Leave enough space between the tables so you can walk around and monitor progress during the learning activities.

If space doesn't allow the use of chevron-style seating, opt for a classroom or U-shape layout. Your main considerations: (1) learners need tables for writing, and (2) they must be able to move into smaller groups for breakout sessions.

Use the checklists included in the course materials to ensure you have all the materials you need and to design a training environment that encourages interaction. The bonus here is that you can speak with personal experience when you recommend the on-site checklist included in the workshop materials to the participants in your class, and even add your own suggestions for additional checklist items.

Presentation skills training is an excellent workshop to use all those extra facilitator tools that we threaten to use, but always seem to put off. Get a good stock of table toys so that the kinesthetic learners have something to occupy their hands so their minds can stay focused. Put up posters and incorporate color into the room for your visual learners' enjoyment. And have music playing when participants enter and during the learning activities for your auditory learners.

All of these ideas are specific concepts that you'll be discussing in the workshop, so you'll be able to offer an example when you get to those sections by showing how you used learning styles in your design of the workshop atmosphere.

Communicating Your Workshop Goals

Communicating the goals of your workshop to the organization and prospective attendees is vital, not only to ensure attendance but also to be sure that attendees know what to expect when they get to the workshop.

The presentation skills workshop you're preparing to conduct is interactive and enjoyable, so let that fact show in your communications. How many class flyers have you seen that are simply a block of black type on white paper? What was your immediate reaction? Did it pique your interest?

What if that same workshop brochure was on vibrantly colored paper with captivating designs and a clever theme? It might just catch your eye and intrigue you. Remember, people decide if they're actually going to read our communications in about 10 seconds, so we need to give those messages all the help we can.

In all communications leading up to the workshop, clearly state the goals and what participants should expect. Remind them of these goals whenever you contact them by email. It's discouraging to everyone involved when a person has an unrealistic idea of what will be covered in a workshop or is not prepared for a session that requires delivering a presentation. Don't put anyone in that situation.

Be willing to promote the workshop at staff and management meetings. Yes, sometimes a trainer has to be a combination of cheerleader and salesperson. Use testimonials from people who've attended the course and followed through with the development of their speaking skills. Testimonials work. (There's a reason every diet pill has someone named Mary telling us how many pounds she lost.)

And, here's one last idea for building interest in your workshops among future attendees: award certificates to graduates. Receiving a certificate reinforces feelings of accomplishment and creates pride in those who've participated.

They'll probably hang the certificates in their cubicles, and a certificate on the wall is seen much more often than a flyer from the training department.

 ## What to Do Next

- ♦   Finalize your goals for the program.

- ♦   Review the on-site checklist (Tool 12–5) to determine the layout and design of your classroom.

- ♦   Create a promotional plan for your workshop.

- ♦   Design and distribute flyers, emails, and information on the program you will present.

- ♦   Set up your timeline for preparing workshop materials.

♦ ♦ ♦

In the first part of this workbook you've been assessing, planning, and coordinating the logistics of your program. In the next chapter you'll change hats and start to prepare for the program as a facilitator.

Facilitating the Workshop

- ◆ Overview of workshop preparations

- ◆ Instructions for preparing participant materials

- ◆ Explanation of the principles of effective facilitation

The term *facilitation* signifies the point at which we go beyond the concept of teaching into the realm of interactive and experiential learning. We all know that learners remember 10 percent of what they hear; 20 percent of what they see; 65 percent of what they hear and see; and 90 percent of what they *hear, see, and do*. This is the principle that drives the activities in your presentation skills workshop. Your learners will be "doing" a lot in the sessions to ensure maximum retention of the skills they practice there.

Workshop Preparations

It's best if you can set up for your workshop the day before the session. This enables you to catch any problems with missing or faulty equipment, and ensures that you're not sweaty and worn out from moving tables and equipment at 8:00 a.m. when your attendees arrive.

Be sure to have set your facilitator table with your instructor's guide and all the hole-punched handouts that you'll give out to the attendees at different points during the workshop. Load your CD player with suitable music and turn on your computer with the Microsoft PowerPoint presentation loaded directly onto the hard drive. Don't play the PowerPoint slides from the website because that slows down the response time and offers more chances for malfunction.

Also, have a supply of basic items for your own convenience—a glass of water is a necessity, mints or breath spray boost confidence, and your favorite headache remedy in case you need it. Once again, I'm speaking from personal experience; outfit yourself with whatever supplies you think you'll need.

Check the markers and flipcharts. You don't want to find you have a dry marker or only two sheets of paper. You'll also want to have dry-erase markers (and know which ones are which), masking tape torn into strips and attached to the back of the flipchart easel so you can post pages around the room, and a timer to keep up with the exercises. A prize bag is an optional item that's always a big hit. Just load it up with rewards from your local dollar store and watch people get into the spirit of competition.

If there's a phone in the room, check to see what you have to do to silence it for the duration of the workshop. Find out how to operate the thermostat. Learn where the light switches are. And ask about fire exits and restroom locations if it's not a building where you normally work.

Be sure the room is set for the appropriate number of attendees. Take a seat in the back row and around the outer edges of the tables to confirm that everyone will have a good view of the screen and of all activity at the front of the room.

When you feel confident that you've addressed all the details of your meeting room, prepare the site for your attendees.

Participant Materials

Set the following materials at each attendee's place:

- ◆ a binder filled with the handouts
- ◆ a few sticky-notes attached to the front of the binders
- ◆ pencil or pen
- ◆ several sheets of paper for note taking
- ◆ a name badge (don't use table tents because your learners move around during this workshop).

Place the following materials on each table for group use:

- markers for activities that require flipcharting

- a few flipchart pages

- snacks, such as hard candies (some sugar-free) and pretzels

- toys or gadgets to keep restless hands busy but not involved enough to distract from the learning activities.

Principles of Effective Facilitation

When you've set the stage, you're ready to move into the world of facilitation. Here are some of the best practices to help guarantee the success of your session:

- One thing that helps take the pressure off is telling participants that *you're* still learning too. Your efforts to improve your facilitation and presentation skills serve as an example to learners and remove one of the barriers that make attendees reluctant to participate. Doing this also releases you from the must-be-perfect expectation (yours or theirs).

- Set ground rules at the beginning of the session. Be sure to turn off your cell phone at the same time you tell them to silence theirs. That's another opportunity to lead by example.

- Use verbal and nonverbal reinforcement techniques to create rapport. Watch for nonverbal cues. Are they fidgeting? Do they look confused? Is anyone dozing off? Are people putting on sweaters? Respond as needed to the cues you get.

- Use appropriate humor as a communication tool, but don't feel it's necessary to tell jokes. Not all of us are meant to be stand-up comedians.

- Keep lecture time to a minimum. If you find that a segment of the workshop is not eliciting enough discussion, modify the format to let the participants teach that section. It's your workshop; you make the rules.

- Count to 10 after you ask a question. One of the big challenges for facilitators is to let a moment of silence pass. Just remember that the participants don't know this material like you do. It takes them a little longer to process the new information, make connections, and respond to your queries.

◆ Check frequently for understanding. Ask your learners if they understand what you're saying or describing. Have them summarize what they think were the main points of the material you presented.

◆ Handle aggressive behavior by remaining calm. Acknowledge and immediately move the focus to problem solving. You can even get the group to help you deal with the problem.

◆ If problem behavior persists, take a break and privately discuss the situation with the disruptive participant. Remember, yours is the final word. You have the right to define the limits of acceptable behavior and to ask a person who is going beyond those limits to leave the workshop.

◆ Incorporate words that appeal to the different learning styles. For your visual learners, use phrases like, "Let's take a look at this." Auditory learners respond well to hearing-oriented phrases like, "How does that sound?" And your kinesthetic learners feel comfortable with phrases like, "How did that exercise feel to you?"

◆ During activities, it's a good idea to walk around and check on your participants. Some people will finish early and start other conversations. Others will struggle to get started. By continually moving between the groups, you can keep everyone focused on the task at hand and ensure they're doing the activity in the way it's intended. Ask questions like, Did any other questions come up over here? What's the hardest thing about this exercise so far? Is this one working for you? Or you can just give encouragement to the groups.

◆ Occasionally you'll want to ask how this information could be useful in their jobs. This reinforces the concept of taking this learning back into the workplace.

◆ If you see people who are staying quiet, try to include them in the discussion on a simple question or directly ask their opinion.

◆ Don't be surprised if you can't answer all your learners' questions. Ask for ideas from the group. Write down the questions you can't answer or have the questioner write it on a sticky-note and put it on a "Parking Lot" flipchart page. Then you can get an answer after the class and distribute the answer to everyone. The good news here is that every question you have to get an answer for is a question you'll know the answer to next time around.

◆ In the sample agendas included in this workbook, I've estimated the blocks of time each section will take. These times will give you a general idea of how far ahead or behind schedule you're running. If you see that you're falling too far behind, make adjustments. You might want to limit discussion and ask participants to put their questions on sticky-notes in the Parking Lot. If you're running too fast, maybe you're not allowing sufficient time for participants to talk. In that case, stop at the next opportunity and ask for questions on what has been discussed thus far.

◆ If you're running out of time in a class, look through the next exercises and see if you can cover that information in a discussion instead of the exercise you've planned.

◆ Make notes of real time required and spent on exercises, activities, and topics. Note these times in the margins of your manual during the class so you can adjust your agenda planning in future workshop presentations.

◆ You can give your learners data. You can show them charts. You can have them read the handouts and complete the exercises. But the best learning that will happen in that room comes from the example that you set with your behavior, your enthusiasm, and your sincere desire to share the information with them. Set the example of a highly motivated professional.

What to Do Next

◆ Review your presentation checklist (Tool 12–4) and your on-site checklist (Tool 12–5), and determine what needs to be done to complete your workshop plans.

◆ Prepare the handouts and purchase all supplies.

◆ Monitor registration and send confirmation emails.

◆ Check the room setup and ensure that all equipment is working properly.

◆ ◆ ◆

The next chapter will help you evaluate the effectiveness of your workshops so you can continue to develop and adjust the sessions to meet the needs of your organization.

Evaluating the Workshop

- Discussion of the benefits of workshop evaluations

- Information on formal and informal evaluation methods

- Review of the criteria to be evaluated

Evaluations, a valuable tool for improving our skills, are often overlooked. In many cases, evaluations are distributed in the last minutes of a session when participants are anxious to leave and unwilling to spend time giving meaningful comments.

In the same way that an unhappy customer is our best tool for enhancing company performance, a participant who has just completed our program is the best barometer of our effectiveness and adequacy.

Additionally, in a class on presentation skills, a presenter's willingness to be evaluated by the attendees sends a strong message. If that facilitator still believes in continual improvement, it reminds the participants that they, too, should be willing to continue developing their abilities.

Formal Evaluation Methods

Most formal evaluation forms include a 1-to-5 scale for rating class content, environment, and facilitation. And such a simple rating often is all that participants will have the time to complete. But adding a few questions to your survey and ensuring that you provide enough time for your learners to give you thoughtful answers can increase the information you receive on these forms.

Here are several sample questions to include:

- ◆ What did you learn from this workshop that you'll be able to use in your job?

- ◆ What would you like more of in this workshop?

- ◆ What would you like less of in this workshop?

If you allow five extra minutes for attendees to complete evaluations, including those questions, you can harvest a great many honest perceptions of the value of your workshops and of your presentation style.

Here are some other ideas for making the most effective use of your evaluation forms.

- ◆ Turn your evaluation form into a pre- and a post-assessment form. For the pre-assessment portion, include these questions:

  1. What is something you know about presentation skills?

  2. What area of presentation skills would you like to learn more about?

  3. How would you rate your skill level in presentation skills?

  For the post-assessment portion, include these questions:

  1. What is something you learned today about presentation skills?

  2. Did you learn anything about the area you cited in pre-assessment question 2?

  3. How would you rate your presentation skill level after this class?

- ◆ Evaluation by class discussion also can be useful if prefaced correctly. It's important to let the participants know that their comments are being accepted in the spirit of development and that you will not be offended or resentful about anything they say.

- ◆ Using a 30-day reminder letter offers an opportunity to build an additional evaluation into your program. This is a simple letter that thanks attendees for participating in the class and asking if there are skills they learned that they are now using in the workplace. You might also adapt the letter and send it to the attendee's supervisor. In this letter you'll ask the supervisor if he or she has noticed an improvement in the employee's skill level. You can also ask the supervisor to visit with the employee and ask what strategies from the workshop he or she has found most useful. This follow-up enables you to see what skills attendees developed as a result of the workshop. This letter is also a chance to gather data that defines your training initiative's return-on-investment—something that the organization's managers will be interested in knowing and something that will help you justify more resources for your program.

♦ Informal evaluations or interviews are also useful tools. These are discussions with attendees or their supervisors to discuss why they came to the workshop and whether that need was addressed. Also using follow-up "alumni sessions" is an effective method to determine if the course has made a difference in the attendees' presentation skills and to offer a few additional pointers to continue development of those skills.

Criteria to Be Evaluated

Here are samples of the basic criteria you'll want to evaluate for any workshops you present. These criteria can be included in survey forms, evaluations, follow-up studies, or classroom discussions:

♦ Participants enjoyed the program.

♦ Participants received the information they needed/wanted.

♦ Activities and methods responsive to the principles of adult learning were built into the course.

♦ The course appealed to visual, auditory, and kinesthetic learners.

♦ Content was relevant to participants' jobs.

♦ The workshop included exercises to practice the new skills that were being taught.

♦ Time spent on practice and feedback was adequate.

♦ Course materials were designed to be used as on-the-job aids.

♦ Learners were motivated to use the new skills back on the job.

- Participants will be able to perform their jobs better as a result of training.

- Facilitator was effective in communicating the materials.

What to Do Next

- Review the agenda for the workshop you'll be presenting.

- Create all handouts and tools from the materials on the accompanying website.

- Determine what formats you'll implement for evaluation and for follow-up.

◆ ◆ ◆

The next chapters present agendas for each of the workshop formats.

One-Hour Program

- ◆ Objectives for the one-hour presentation skills workshop

- ◆ Lists of materials for facilitator and participants

- ◆ Detailed program agenda to be used as a facilitator's guide

The one-hour workshop is an introduction to the importance of presentation skills and their benefits to the workplace. Attendees will practice a short presentation with a partner and receive feedback on the effectiveness of that presentation. They also will create action plans for continued development.

Training Objectives

The participants' objectives for the one-hour presentation skills workshop are to

- ◆ identify the benefits of presentation skills

- ◆ get an introduction to the formula for impromptu speaking

- ◆ create a plan to develop their presentation skills.

Materials

For the facilitator:

- ◆ This chapter for reference and use as a facilitator guide

- ◆ Learning Activity 11–1: Introductions

- Learning Activity 11–8: The S-E-T Formula

- PowerPoint slide program, titled "Presentation Skills" (slides 7–1 through 7–9). To access slides for this program, open the file *One-Hour.ppt* on the accompanying website. Thumbnail versions of the slides for this two-day workshop are included at the end of this chapter.

- Projector, screen, and computer for displaying PowerPoint slides; alternatively, overhead transparencies and overhead projector

For the participants:

- Copies of all the slides in the PowerPoint presentation, printed three per page

- Assessment 12–1: Self-Assessment

- Assessment 12–2: Program Evaluation

- Training Instrument 12–1: Introductions

- Training Instrument 12–8: The S-E-T Formula

- Index cards

- *Optional:* assorted snacks or candies (some sugar-free) in cups

DOWNLOADS

Using the Website

Materials for the training session are provided in this workbook and as electronic files on the accompanying website. To access the electronic files, go to the website and click on the appropriate Adobe .pdf document. Further directions and help using the files can be found in the appendix titled "Using the Website" at the back of this workbook.

It's important that you review all of the slides as part of your preparation for the workshop. As you review them, plan explanations and examples for concepts presented in the slides.

Workshop Preparation

Before the class begins, set the room with the following items:

- PowerPoint slide 7–1

- flipchart and markers

- participant handouts at each seat

- pencils or pens

- blank paper for each participant

- name badge for each participant

- assorted snacks and candies, as desired.

Sample Agenda

The times assigned to the elements of this training are approximate and will vary with discussion and facilitator emphasis. The times of the exercises can be adjusted to fit your available time slot.

8:00 a.m.   Welcome and Agenda (3 minutes)

Introduce yourself and the purpose of the workshop. Go over the ground rules for the session. Here are some sample ground rules and housekeeping items:

- Turn cell phones to silent.

- Because this workshop is interactive, be prepared to participate!

- Respectful communication is required. If someone is speaking, all attention should be given to that person.

Show slide 7–2. Review the objectives. Show slide 7–3 and go through the agenda items. Ask for any questions.

8:03   Introductions (15 minutes)

Show slide 7–4. Distribute Training Instrument 12–1. Perform Learning Activity 11–1, adjusting the time to 15 minutes. Point out that we're called on to do presentations every day, just like the introductions performed in the activity. Ask learners if their meetings would go more smoothly if everyone had the ability to present more concisely and effectively. Ask what other benefits they feel good presentation skills would bring to the workplace.

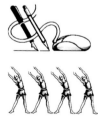

8:18   Self-Assessments (10 minutes)

Show slide 7–5 and distribute Assessment 12–1. Ask learners to complete this assessment individually. Assure them that the answers they give are for their eyes only, so they can be completely candid.

When everyone is finished, briefly discuss the assessment. Ask if they discovered areas that they would like to develop. Ask if they are more comfortable with planned or with impromptu speaking. Did they find their biggest challenge is writing presentations or presenting them?

On slide 7–5, click the mouse to reveal the four types of presenter as you explain each one. Ask if participants recognize themselves.

- ◆ **Avoiders:** those who avoid speaking at all

- ◆ **Resisters:** those who resist speaking, but can do it if forced

- ◆ **Reluctants:** those who don't mind speaking, but don't seek out opportunities

- ◆ **Enthusiasts:** those who actively seek opportunities to speak.

8:28   Impromptu Speaking (15 minutes)

Just as in the introductions exercise, we're often called to give impromptu talks. Explain that in this workshop you'll show them a formula they can use to immediately organize their thoughts for these types of presentations.

Show slide 7–6. The S-E-T Formula is a simple method for speakers to organize their thoughts when they're asked to make an impromptu presentation. Here are the three factors in the formula:

- ◆ **S = short answer.** Give the bottom-line answer first.

- ◆ **E = evidence supporting the answer.** Elaborate a little by giving the evidence and why it supports the short answer.

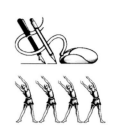

- **T = transition.** Here the speaker summarizes and transitions to the next point or person.

Distribute Training Instrument 12–8. Perform Learning Activity 11–8.

The "elevator speech" is one example of a presentation for which participants can use the S-E-T Formula.

8:43   Elevator Speech (5 minutes)

Show slide 7–7. Explain that elevator speeches are based on this idea: What if there were someone you've been trying to meet with and you find yourself on the elevator with that person? You have only a few floors to get an idea across to this person. An elevator speech can fulfill that need. It's a brief talk on a subject that's important to the speaker. It should last no more than 30 seconds so it actually can be told in the span of an elevator ride, and it should include the basic points that are important for the listener to know about the topic.

Remind participants that it's an excellent idea to rehearse elevator speeches on all of their current projects. Then, when they find themselves in situations where they need to present this information briefly and concisely, they're ready to make the most of the opportunity.

Here's an example of an instant project update using the S-E-T formula: Your manager asks, "How's that ABC project going?" You answer

- **S:** *It's right on schedule.*

- **E:** *We've completed phases 1 and 2 and we'll start phase 3 on Monday. We anticipate having the draft of the project on your desk at the end of next week.*

- **T:** *Does that work for you?*

8:48   Action Plan (5 minutes)

Show slide 7–8. Hand out index cards to all participants and ask them to write two things on the card:

          1. a process they learned today that they'll teach within 24 hours.

          2. a topic they're often called on to speak about in the workplace.

Instruct them to create an elevator speech on this topic within the next week.

8:53   Program Evaluation (2 minutes)

Distribute Assessment 12–2. Reinforce the idea of continual development by asking for their input on the evaluation form. When you show your commitment to your own continued skill development, you demonstrate that this should be an ongoing process for them as well.

8:55   Close (5 minutes)

Show slide 7–9. Ask for questions. Remind attendees of the date set for the next full presentation skills workshop. Leave them with a parting joke, quote, or inspirational comment.

What to Do Next

- ◆ Using the material in chapter 4 as a guide, build a detailed plan to prepare for this session.

- ◆ Schedule a meeting room and invite your attendees.

- ◆ Draft a supply list, teaching notes, and time estimates.

- ◆ Decide how you will support the action plan for the learners.

- ◆ Follow each of the steps of your workshop plan to prepare and present your program.

- ◆ Evaluate the effectiveness of the program, using the ideas from chapter 6.

- ◆ Consider designing follow-up sessions to encourage the learners to continue developing presentation skills.

Slide 7–1

Slide 7–2

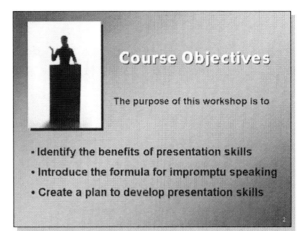

Slide 7–3

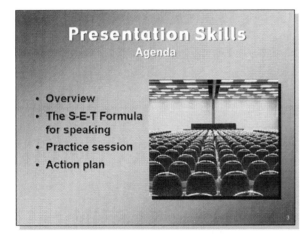

Slide 7–4

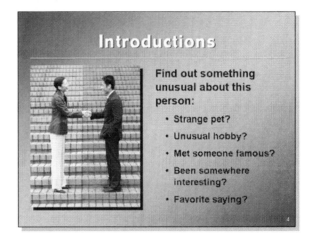

Slide 7–5

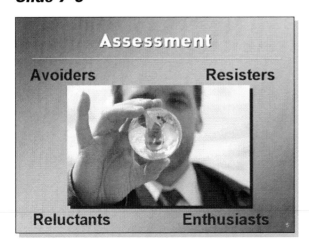

Slide 7–6

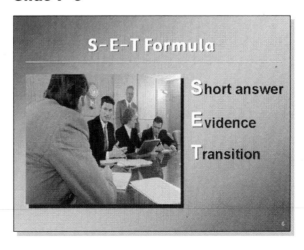

Slide 7–7

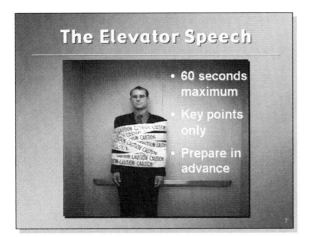

Slide 7–8

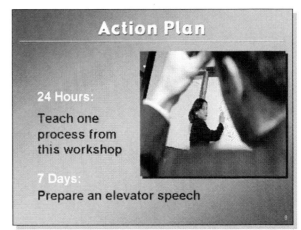

Slide 7–9

Chapter 8

Half-Day Program

What's in This Chapter?

- Objectives for the half-day presentation skills workshop
- Lists of materials for facilitator and participants
- Detailed program agenda to be used as a facilitator's guide

The half-day workshop provides time for learners to discover the process of planning, designing, and writing effective presentations. This workshop also enables participants to deliver short presentations to build their confidence in presenting. Learners receive feedback from their peers and create action plans for continued development.

Training Objectives

The objectives for the half-day presentation skills workshop are to

- design presentations that inform, instruct, persuade, or inspire an audience
- adapt presentations to accommodate the needs of different audiences
- study presentation methods that keep audiences engaged.

Materials

For the facilitator:

- This chapter for reference and use as a facilitator guide
- Learning Activity 11–1: Introductions

- Learning Activity 11–8: The S-E-T Formula

- Learning Activity 11–9: S-E-T Practice Session

- Learning Activity 11–18: Action Plan

- PowerPoint slide program titled "Presentation Skills" (slides 8–1 through 8–14). To access slides for this program, open the file *Half-Day.ppt* on the accompanying website. Thumbnail versions of the slides for this half-day workshop are included at the end of this chapter.

- Projector, screen, and computer for displaying PowerPoint slides; alternatively, overhead transparencies and overhead projector

For the participants:

- Copies of all the slides in the PowerPoint presentation, printed three per page; one set of handouts for each learner, three-hole punched and placed in a binder

- Assorted toys scattered on the tables to help kinesthetic learners occupy their hands and increase their concentration while listening to discussions

- Assessment 12–1: Self-Assessment

- Assessment 12–2: Program Evaluation

- Tool 12–2: Presentation Planning Form

- Tool 12–8: Guidelines for Visual Aids

- Training Instrument 12–1: Introductions

- Training Instrument 12–6: Guidelines for Preparing a Presentation Planning Form

- Training Instrument 12–8: The S-E-T Formula

- Training Instrument 12–15: Continued Development Action Plan

- Training Instrument 12–16: Practice Session

- *Optional:* assorted snacks or candies (some sugar-free) in cups on the tables

Using the Website

DOWNLOADS

Materials for the training session are provided in this workbook and as electronic files on the accompanying website. To access the electronic files, go to the website and click on the appropriate Adobe .pdf document. Further directions and help using the files can be found in the appendix titled "Using the Website" at the back of this workbook.

It's important that you review all of the slides as part of your preparation for the workshop. As you review them, plan explanations and examples for concepts presented in the slides.

Workshop Preparation

Before the class begins, set the room with the following items:

- ♦ PowerPoint slide 8–1

- ♦ posted agenda

- ♦ binder with participants' handouts at each seat

- ♦ sticky-notes attached to each binder

- ♦ pencils or pens

- ♦ blank paper for each participant

- ♦ name badge for each participant

- ♦ assorted snacks and candies, as desired.

Sample Agenda

The times assigned to the elements of this training are approximate and will vary with discussion and facilitator emphasis.

8:00 a.m.   Welcome (5 minutes)

Introduce yourself and the purpose of the workshop. Go over the ground rules for the session. Here are some sample ground rules and housekeeping items:

- ♦ Turn cell phones to silent.

- ♦ Because this workshop is interactive, be prepared to participate!

♦ Restrooms, smoking areas, snacks, and vending machines are located in the following areas: *[add details].*

♦ Respectful communication is required. If someone is speaking, all attention should be given to that person.

8:05   Objectives (5 minutes)

Show slide 8–2. Review the workshop objectives.

8:10   Agenda (5 minutes)

Show slide 8–3. Go through the agenda items and ask for any questions.

8:15   Introductions (20 minutes)

Show slide 8–4. Distribute Training Instrument 12–1. Perform the activity as described in Learning Activity 11–1. These introductions and the discussion set the stage for the following assessment of presentation skills comfort levels.

8:35   Self-Assessments (10 minutes)

Show slide 8–5. Distribute Assessment 12–1. Ask learners to complete this assessment individually. Assure them that the answers they give are for their eyes only, so they can be completely candid.

When everyone is finished, briefly discuss the questions on the assessment. Ask if they discovered areas that they would like to develop. Ask if they are more comfortable with planned speaking or with impromptu speaking. Did they find that their biggest challenge is writing presentations or presenting them? Discuss how today's workshop will help in each of those areas.

8:45   Types of Presentations (5 minutes)

Show slide 8–6. Ask learners to call out reasons they are asked to give speeches and presentations. Write these reasons on a flipchart page. (If you have an attendee who looks anxious to get involved, ask that person to be your scribe and to do the writing for you.) If necessary, start with your own examples, such as reporting on project progress in staff meetings and explaining new office procedures.

Explain the following four types of presentations. Ask learners to help you link each of their samples to the type of presentation they think it would be. Underline each type in a different color.

Click on slide 8–6 to reveal each type of presentation as you discuss it:

- ◆ **Informational:** This is one type of presentation we do quite often. Its purpose is to give information to the group—a project update, a new employee orientation, or a book report.

- ◆ **Instructional:** This is an easy one. Ask them where they are today. Workshops and training classes are examples of instructional presentations. These presentations teach and demonstrate how to do processes.

- ◆ **Persuasive:** This type of presentation seeks to initiate action and can include anything from a political candidate's speech to a talk about home security systems to a neighborhood watch committee. Its purpose is to influence the audience to adopt a particular point of view or take some action.

- ◆ **Inspirational:** This type of presentation seeks to create certain feelings in the audience, to motivate or lift the spirits of the audience. Religious, motivational, and even some purely entertaining speeches can be inspirational.

8:50   Impromptu Speaking (20 minutes)

Show slide 8–7. Ask for examples of times when participants are called on to do impromptu speaking and what types of topics they're asked to address.

Show slide 8–8. The S-E-T Formula is a simple method for speakers to organize their thoughts when they're asked to make an impromptu presentation. Here are the three factors in the formula:

- ◆ **S = short answer.** Give the bottom-line answer first.

- ◆ **E = evidence supporting the answer.** Elaborate a little by giving the evidence and why it supports the short answer.

- ◆ **T = transition.** Here the speaker summarizes and transitions to the next point or person.

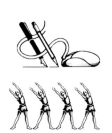

Distribute Training Instrument 12–8. Perform the activity as described in Learning Activity 11–8.

The S-E-T Formula also can be used to construct each section of a longer presentation. It's a formula that keeps the speaker focused as she or he explains or addresses each point in a talk. The "elevator speech" uses this formula.

9:10   Elevator Speech (10 minutes)

Show slide 8–9. Explain that elevator speeches are based on this idea: What if there were someone you've been trying to meet with and you find yourself on the elevator with that person? You have only a few floors to get an idea across to this person. An elevator speech can fulfill that need. It's a brief talk on a subject that's important to the speaker. It should last no more than 30 seconds so it actually can be told in the span of an elevator ride, and it should include the basic points that are important for the listener to know about the topic.

Remind participants that it's an excellent idea to rehearse elevator speeches on all of their current projects. Then, when they find themselves in situations where they need to present this information briefly and concisely, they're ready to make the most of the opportunity.

Here's an example of an instant project update using the S-E-T formula: Your manager asks, "How's that ABC project going?" You answer

- ◆ **S:** *It's right on schedule.*

- ◆ **E:** *We've completed phases 1 and 2 and we'll start phase 3 on Monday. We anticipate having the draft of the project on your desk at the end of next week.*

- ◆ **T:** *Does that work for you?*

9:20   Break (15 minutes)

9:35   S-E-T Practice Session (75 minutes)

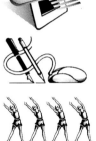

Show slide 8–10 and distribute Training Instrument 12–16. Explain that learners are going to get a chance to practice an impromptu presentation. Perform Learning Activity 11–9, using Training Instrument 12–16 and the questions on slide 8–10.

10:50°   Constructing the Presentation (30 minutes)

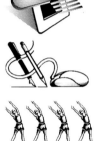

Show slide 8–11. Pass out Training Instrument 12–6. Explain that creating presentations is as simple as *Get Ready, Get Set, Go:*

- ◆ **Get Ready** stands for the planning phase of presentation design. This includes the brainstorming and research stages of a presentation.

- ◆ **Get Set** is the next phase. It consists of organizing the information gathered into a cohesive whole, using the *S-E-T formula.*

- ◆ **Go** is the actual writing phase of presentation design.

Go through each of the following blanks on Tool 12–2: Presentation Planning Form.

- ◆ **Topic:** List your basic topic of discussion.

- ◆ **Date:** Insert the date of the presentation.

- ◆ **Time:** Note the time your presentation will begin and end.

♦ **Event/Theme:** Indicate if this presentation is part of a larger event. Define the overall theme of that event.

♦ **Attendees:** Write the number of people expected.

♦ **Location:** Insert the exact address and room number for your presentation.

♦ **Room Setup:** How will the chairs be set?

11:20   Parts of the Presentation (20 minutes)

Continuing with the sections of the Presentation Planning Form, discuss the remaining portions:

♦ **Opening:** Ask the group to suggest ideas for openings and write them on the flipchart. Examples of good openings include rhetorical questions, startling statistics, quotations, anecdotes, surveys, and humor. Discuss some of your favorite sources for opening materials, including current websites.

♦ **Point One, Point Two, and Point Three:** Using three main points is a good standard to start with because surveys have shown that listeners tend to be able to retain that number of points. Of course, whether a three-point structure will work for your audience depends on the topic. The most important thing to keep in mind is that attention span we discussed earlier. If an audience is overloaded with data, they'll stop listening.

♦ **Review and Restate:** Explain that this is the part of the presentation where they'll summarize by reviewing and restating the information and flowing straight into the closing.

♦ **First Closing:** Note that many of the same items that learners used for introductions are appropriate choices for closings too.

♦ **Question-and-Answer Period:** This section will be used for presentations that include a time for questions from the audience. This is where the speaker should consider the topic and the audience, and then list questions that might be asked.

◆ **Second Closing:** This is a great secret of seasoned presenters. Novice speakers often complete the Q&A segment with a whimper instead of a bang—just sort of drifting off. The impact of even the most inspiring closing statement is lost in that drift. Having a second closing prepared lets the speaker end the Q&A with power. Use the same rules for this closing as for the first closing, and create a statement that reinforces the presentation's purpose one last time.

11:40   Visual Aids (15 minutes)

Show slide 8–12. Most learners are visual learners. For this reason, using visual aids has become a major factor in creating successful presentations. Hand out Tool 12–8.

11:55   Action Plan (10 minutes)

Show slide 8–13. Distribute Training Instrument 12–15. Perform Learning Activity 11–18. Participants will fill out the commitment form and share it with a partner in the class for follow-up.

12:05 p.m.   Program Evaluation (5 minutes)

Distribute Assessment 12–2. Reinforce the idea of continual development by asking for their input on the evaluation form. When you show your commitment to your own continued skill development, you demonstrate that this should be an ongoing process for them as well.

12:10   Review and Closing (10 minutes)

Ask for questions. Ask participants to share some ideas from the session that they'll be able to apply back in the workplace. Finally, using one of your favorite quotes or stories, close the program as you have told them to do—with a great flourish.

What to Do Next

♦   Using the material in chapter 4 as a guide, build a detailed plan to prepare for this workshop.

♦   Schedule a training room and invite your attendees.

♦   Draft a supply list, teaching notes, and time estimates.

♦   Decide how you will support the action plan to which your learners will commit.

♦   Follow each of the steps of your workshop plan to prepare and present your program.

♦   Evaluate the effectiveness of the program, using the ideas from chapter 6.

♦   Consider designing follow-up sessions to encourage the learners to continue developing presentation skills.

Slide 8–1

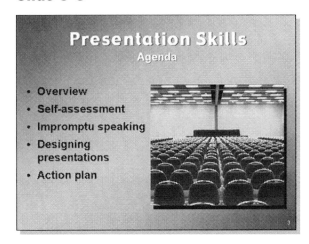

Slide 8–2

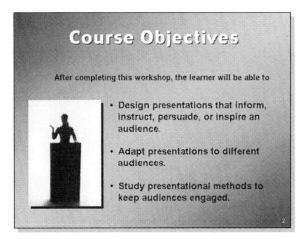

Slide 8–3

Slide 8–4

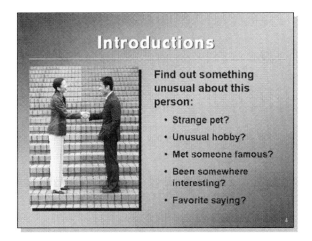

Slide 8–5

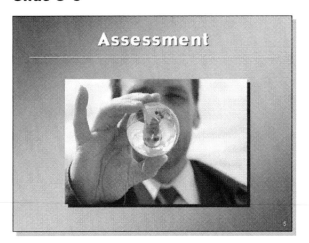

Slide 8–6

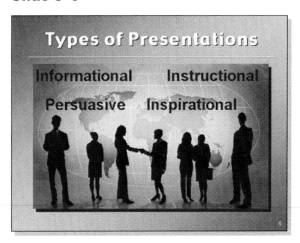

Slide 8–7

Slide 8–8

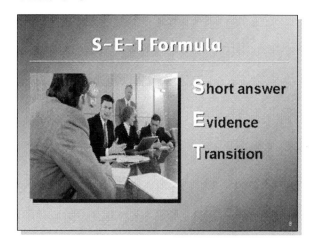

Slide 8–9

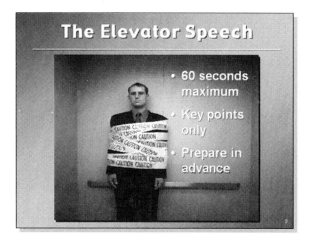

Slide 8–10

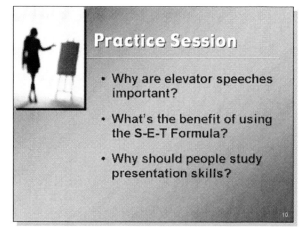

Slide 8–11

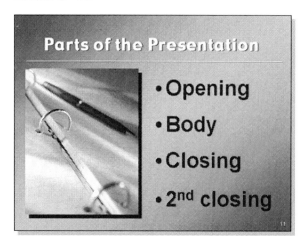

Slide 8–12

Slide 8–13

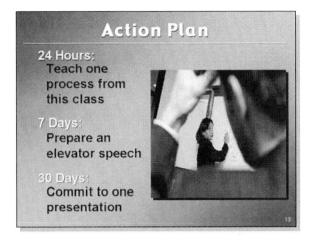

Slide 8–14

One-Day Program

- Objectives for the one-day presentation skills workshop

- Lists of materials for facilitator and participants

- Detailed program agenda to be used as a facilitator's guide

The one-day workshop allows learners to discover the processes of planning, designing, and writing effective presentations. This workshop also enables participants to deliver various types of presentations so that they build their confidence in presenting. Learners receive feedback from their peers and create action plans for continued development.

Training Objectives

The participants' objectives for the one-day presentation skills workshop are to

- design presentations that inform, instruct, persuade, or inspire

- adapt presentations to accommodate the needs of different audiences

- become familiar with presentation methods to keep audiences engaged.

Materials

For the facilitator:

- This chapter for reference and use as a facilitator guide

- Learning Activity 11–1: Introductions

- Learning Activity 11–8: The S-E-T Formula

- Learning Activity 11–9: S-E-T Practice Session

- Learning Activity 11–13: Visual Aids

- Learning Activity 11–15: Challenging Situations

- Learning Activity 11–16: Presentation Practice Session

- Learning Activity 11–17: Speaking Opportunities

- Learning Activity 11–18: Action Plan

- PowerPoint slide program, titled "Presentation Skills" (slides 9–1 through 9–23). To access slides for this program, open the file *One-Day.ppt* on the accompanying website. Thumbnail versions of the slides for this one-day workshop are included at the end of this chapter.

- Projector, screen, and computer for displaying PowerPoint slides; alternatively, overhead transparencies and overhead projector

- *Optional:* Video camera

For the participants:

- Copies of all the slides in the PowerPoint presentation, printed three per page; one set of handouts for each learner, three-hole punched and placed in a binder

- One flipchart and four markers for each group of four participants

- Assessment 12–1: Self-Assessment

- Assessment 12–2: Program Evaluation

- Assessment 12–4: Presenter Evaluation

- Tool 12–2: Presentation Planning Form

- Tool 12–3: Pre-Presentation Questionnaire

- Tool 12–6: Tips for Delivering Presentations

- Tool 12–8: Guidelines for Visual Aids

- Training Instrument 12–1: Introductions

- Training Instrument 12–5: Overcoming Nervousness

- Training Instrument 12–6: Guidelines for Preparing a Presentation Planning Form

- Training Instrument 12–8: The S-E-T Formula

- Training Instrument 12–9: S-E-T Practice

- Training Instrument 12–13: Challenging Situations

- Training Instrument 12–14: Practice Session Planning Form

- Training Instrument 12–15: Continued Development Action Plan

- Assorted toys scattered on the tables to help kinesthetic learners occupy their hands and increase their concentration while listening to discussions

- *Optional:* assorted snacks or candies (some sugar-free) in cups

- *Optional:* one blank videotape for each participant

Using the Website

DOWNLOADS

Materials for the training session are provided in this workbook and as electronic files on the accompanying website. To access the electronic files, go to the website and click on the appropriate Adobe .pdf document. Further directions and help using the files can be found in the appendix titled "Using the Website" at the back of this workbook.

It's important that you review all of the slides as part of your preparation for the workshop. As you review them, plan explanations and examples for concepts presented in the slides.

Workshop Preparation

Before the class begins, set the room with the following items:

- flipchart titled "What I Need From Today's Session Is . . . "

- PowerPoint slide 9–1

- posted agenda for the day, which includes the lunch break

- binder with participants' handouts at each seat

- sticky-notes attached to each binder

- pencils or pens

- blank paper for each participant

- name badge for each participant

- assorted snacks and candies, as desired.

 ## Sample Agenda

The times assigned to the elements of this training are approximate and will vary with discussion and facilitator emphasis.

8:00 a.m.   Welcome (10 minutes)

As participants enter the room, welcome them and ask them to write on a sticky-note one thing that they'd like to get from this workshop on presentation skills. When they've written their notes, instruct them to go up and affix them to the flipchart page displayed at the front of the room.

Introduce yourself and the purpose of the workshop. Go over the ground rules for the session. Here are some sample ground rules and housekeeping items:

- Turn cell phones to silent.

- Because this workshop is interactive, be prepared to participate!

- There will be scheduled breaks in the morning and afternoon.

- Lunch break will be one hour.

- Restrooms, smoking areas, snacks, and vending machines are located in the following areas: *[add details]*.

- Respectful communication is required. If someone is speaking, all attention should be given to that person.

If participants don't know the area, it's a good idea to have maps to nearby restaurants or menus they can use to order lunch.

8:10   Objectives (5 minutes)

Show slide 9–2. Review Objectives.

8:15   Agenda (5 minutes)

Show slide 9–3. Go through the agenda items and ask for any questions.

8:20   Participant Goals (5 minutes)

Show slide 9–4. Read the sticky-notes from the flipchart and assure attendees that the program will address those topics. If any of the topics listed won't be brought up, you can add them to the question-and-answer (Q&A) period at the end of the workshop.

8:25   Introductions (25 minutes)

Show slide 9–5. Distribute Training Instrument 12–1. Perform the activity as described in Learning Activity 11–1. These introductions and the discussion set the stage for the following assessment of presentation skills comfort levels.

8:50   Self-Assessments (20 minutes)

Show slide 9–6. Distribute Assessment 12–1. Ask learners to complete this assessment individually. Assure them that the answers they give are for their eyes only, so they can be completely candid.

When everyone is finished, briefly discuss the questions on the assessment. Ask if they discovered areas that they would like to develop. Ask if they are more comfortable with planned speaking or with impromptu speaking. Did they find that their biggest challenge is writing presentations or presenting them? Discuss how today's workshop will help in each of those areas.

On slide 9–6, click the mouse to reveal each type of presenter as you discuss it.

◆ **Avoiders:** those who avoid speaking at all

◆ **Resisters:** those who resist speaking, but can do it if forced

- ◆ **Reluctants:** those who don't mind speaking, but don't seek out opportunities

- ◆ **Enthusiasts:** those who actively seek opportunities to speak.

After you've explained all four groups, use the following lighthearted approach to identify the comfort level of individual attendees. Doing this ensures that no one is embarrassed and gives you an opportunity to see which participants might need extra encouragement.

Explain that this is an "informal" assessment of each person's presenter type. Ask for a show of hands in response to these questions:

1. Who would rather have a root canal than be asked to give a speech? You're our *avoiders.*

2. Who would prefer to be sitting in the back of the room enjoying the presentation, but could speak if absolutely necessary? You're our *resisters.*

3. Who really doesn't mind speaking in front of a group, but can think of a lot of things you'd rather do? You're our *reluctants.*

4. Who lives for captive audiences? Who wants to turn around to others in the elevator and say, "I suppose you wonder why I've called this meeting"? You are our *enthusiasts.*

9:10   Types of Presentations (5 minutes)

Show slide 9–7. Remind participants that, just as there are different types of speakers, there are different types of presentations.

Tell learners to call out reasons they are asked to give speeches and presentations. Write these reasons on a flip-chart page. (If you have an attendee who looks anxious to get involved, ask that person to be your scribe and to do the writing for you.) If necessary, start with your own examples, such as reporting on project progress in staff meetings and explaining new procedures in the office.

Explain the following four types of presentations. Ask learners to help you link their samples to the type of presentation they think it would be. Underline each type in a different color.

Click on slide 9–7 to reveal each type of presentation as you discuss it:

- **Informational:** This is one type of presentation we do quite often. Its purpose is to give information to the group—a project update, a new employee orientation, or a book report.

- **Instructional:** This is an easy one. Ask them where they are today. Workshops and training classes are examples of instructional presentations. Instructional presentations teach and demonstrate how to do processes.

- **Persuasive:** This type of presentation seeks to initiate action and can include anything from a political candidate's speech to a talk about home security systems to a neighborhood watch committee. Its purpose is to influence the audience to adopt a particular point of view or take some action.

- **Inspirational:** This type of presentation seeks to create certain feelings in the audience, to motivate or lift the spirits of the audience.

9:15   Overcoming Nervousness (20 minutes)

Show slide 9–8. Lead into this discussion by noting that, during any of these types of presentations, a speaker may experience the body language of knocking knees, shaking hands, and sweating palms. Ask what these signs indicate.

These physical responses are some of the signs of fear. Remind learners that anyone who experiences these responses is not alone. We've all heard of the survey that found public speaking to be Americans' number-one fear. Even seasoned speakers may grow anxious when preparing to stand in front of a group. This anxiety shows they still care about getting their messages across to the audience. That concern is a good thing!

So how do they conquer that fear? Explain that learners' best ideas for handling any stressful situations can be useful for presentation anxiety. Ask for their ideas on how to handle presentation anxiety. Pass out copies of Training Instrument 12–5.

Click on slide 9–8 to show other examples. Follow up with any items on the slide that were not covered by the group.

- ◆ **Breathe:** Invite participants to take a deep breath. Hold it to a count of four. Then release the breath, counting slowly from eight down to one. Slowing the breathing like this replicates calm breathing and can help trick the mind into a more relaxed disposition.

- ◆ **Practice, practice, practice:** We've all heard the answer to the question, How do I get to Carnegie Hall? "Practice, practice, practice." Remind learners that this is great advice, whether they're trying to overcome fear or to present better speeches. It's also the way they'll nip those negative habits like the irritating "uhs" that punctuate sentences or the jingling of coins in a pocket. Suggest that they practice a presentation until they're sure they have it right. Then practice some more.

- ◆ **Connect with audience:** Ask learners if they felt more comfortable talking to their groups in this exercise than they did in the first exercise of the day. Explain that connecting with their listeners can help them when they're speaking to an audience. Suggest that they learn about the audience before the day of the presentation, and that they arrive early to visit with audience members before the presentation. It's easier to talk to a group when there are some familiar faces in the audience.

It's also possible to establish connections with listeners *during* presentations. A speaker can ask the audience questions, connect with eye contact, and use icebreaker exercises or ask people to introduce themselves. Any of these actions can help lower a speaker's level of nervousness.

◆ **Focus on the message:** Concentrating on the message that one is trying to get across—instead of on one's appearance and on what the audience is thinking—is a great way to relieve the pressure of speaking. As the presenter stands to speak, she or he should hold a quick internal pep rally to highlight the reasons why it's important to get this point across. Focusing on the main theme of the message and how it will benefit the listeners not only helps build confidence, but also boosts the speaker's enthusiasm level.

◆ **Perform practice exercises:** Try a visualization exercise. Some people take a photo of the room where they're going to present their program so they can practice with the photo in front of them. When they get into the room, it's like they've practiced there dozens of times before. Spending a few minutes alone, meditating or practicing breathing and visualizing a successful presentation, can do wonders to counteract the jitters.

To illustrate additional ideas for this calming process, ask the class to try this simple exercise for nerves: Have them put their hands down and grip each side of their chair seats. Tell them to tighten every muscle, hold them tense for 8 seconds, then release. Ask if they feel the difference. Doing this immediately before standing up to deliver a presentation can help relieve tension.

Vocal exercises are excellent preparation if speakers have a private area available to them. They can repeat some of the standard tongue-twister phrases like "rubber baby buggy bumper" or do face stretches to get loosened up.

Summarize this portion of the workshop by distributing Tool 12–6 and noting that these tips for delivering presentations also can help them overcome nervousness about speaking. Explain that, when they come back from the break, you'll help them gain even more confidence by sharing the simplest formula for creating any type of presentation.

9:35   Break (15 minutes)

9:50   Impromptu Speaking (20 minutes)

Show slide 9–9. Ask for examples of times when participants are called on to do impromptu speaking and what types of topics they're asked to address.

Show slide 9–10. The S-E-T Formula is a simple method for speakers to organize their thoughts when they're asked to make an impromptu presentation. Here are the three factors in the formula:

- ◆ **S = short answer.** Give the bottom-line answer first.

- ◆ **E = evidence supporting the answer.** Elaborate a little by giving the evidence and why it supports the short answer.

- ◆ **T = transition.** Here the speaker summarizes and transitions to the next point or person.

Distribute Training Instrument 12–8. Show slide 9–11. Perform Learning Activity 11–8 to enable participants to practice the S-E-T Formula with a partner.

The S-E-T Formula also can be used to construct each section of a longer presentation. It's a formula that keeps the speaker focused as she or he explains or addresses each point in a talk. The "elevator speech" uses this formula.

10:10   Elevator Speech (10 minutes)

Show slide 9–12. Explain that elevator speeches are based on this idea: What if there were someone you've been trying to meet with and you find yourself on the elevator with that person? You have only a few floors to get an idea across to this person. An elevator speech can fulfill that need. It's a brief talk on a subject that's important to the speaker. It should last no more than 30 seconds so it actually can be told in the span of an elevator ride, and it should include the basic points that are important for the listener to know about the topic.

Remind participants that it's an excellent idea to rehearse elevator speeches on all of their current projects. Then, when they find themselves in situations where they need to present this information briefly and concisely, they're ready to make the most of the opportunity.

Here's an example of an instant project update using the S-E-T formula: Your manager asks, "How's that ABC project going?" You answer

- ♦ **S:** *It's right on schedule.*

- ♦ **E:** *We've completed phases 1 and 2 and we'll start phase 3 on Monday. We anticipate having the draft of the project on your desk at the end of next week.*

- ♦ **T:** *Does that work for you?*

10:20   Practice Session (75 minutes)

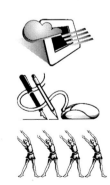

Show slide 9–13 and distribute Training Instrument 12–16. Explain that learners are going to get a chance to practice an impromptu presentation. Distribute Training Instrument 12–9. Perform Learning Activity 11–9.

11:35   Lunch (60 minutes)

12:35 p.m.   Review (15 minutes)

Perform Learning Activity 11–17, replacing the topic of speaking opportunities by having learners give one piece of information they've learned in the session as they toss the beach ball to one another.

12:50   Designing Presentations (30 minutes)

Show slide 9–14. Pass out Training Instrument 12–6. Explain that creating presentations is as simple as *Get Ready, Get Set, Go:*

◆ **Get Ready** stands for the planning phase of presentation design. This includes the brainstorming and research stages of a presentation.

◆ **Get Set** is the next phase. It consists of organizing the information gathered into a cohesive whole, using the *S-E-T formula.*

◆ **Go** is the actual writing phase of presentation design.

Refer participants to Training Instrument 12–6, instructing them to use this to make notes about the steps of preparation. Distribute Tool 12–2 and explain that this is a blank form they can keep, copy, and use whenever they need to plan a presentation.

Describe how to complete each of the following blanks on the Presentation Planning Form:

◆ **Topic:** List your basic topic of discussion.

◆ **Date:** Insert the date of the presentation.

◆ **Time:** Note the time your presentation will begin and end.

◆ **Event/Theme:** Indicate if this presentation is part of a larger event. Define the overall theme of that event.

◆ **Attendees:** Write the number of people expected.

- **Location:** Insert the exact address and room number for your presentation.

- **Room Setup:** Describe how the chairs and tables will be arranged.

- **Purpose:** Show slide 9–15 and explain that the purpose of a presentation is the ultimate reason for which you're making the presentation—that is, essentially ensuring that the audience knows something, does something, or feels something when the presentation is over. Ask if participants remember the four types of presentations you discussed earlier. The type broadly identifies the purpose: Informational and instructional presentations help the listener know or do something; persuasive presentations encourage the listener to take an action; inspirational presentations are meant to prompt feelings in the listener. No matter which goal a speaker has in mind, here's a good rule of thumb: if you can't state the purpose of the presentation in a single sentence, you haven't defined the topic well enough.

  Ask participants to try stating the purpose of today's workshop in one sentence. Let them come up with their own purpose statements for the class. All their statements will be valid because they present what the individual listener needs and hopes to get from the class.

- **Audience Notes:** Show slide 9–16 and distribute Tool 12–3. An analysis of the anticipated audience is the part of the preparation process that directs speakers to find out about the group they'll be addressing.

  Ask participants what things they'd like to know about their audiences. Write their answers on a flipchart page. Sample answers might include the average age of the attendees, their average educational level, whether the group will be hostile to the idea being presented, whether listeners are expecting to be entertained or to be informed, and what the audience already knows about the topic. These are the things speakers want to know so they can be sure to include a good dose of *what's in it for me?* in the introduction. The audience members need to understand what they're going to gain from listening; otherwise, they won't be engaged in the presentation.

To help your participants see how making notes about the audience helps them craft a presentation, first give them these specifics: *You are giving a presentation on time management to a group of 25-year-olds who don't think that time management is important to them.* Next, ask them for examples of how this audience profile would affect the way they present the information.

1:20   Parts of the Presentation (20 minutes)

Continuing with the sections of the Presentation Planning Form, discuss the remaining portions:

- ◆ **Opening:** Show slide 9–17. Ask the group to suggest ideas for openings and write them on the flipchart. Examples of good openings include rhetorical questions, startling statistics, quotations, anecdotes, surveys, and humor. Discuss some of your favorite sources for opening materials, including current websites.

- ◆ **Point One, Point Two, and Point Three:** Using three main points is a good standard to start with because surveys have shown that listeners tend to be able to retain that number of points. Of course, whether a three-point structure will work for your audience depends on the topic. The most important thing to keep in mind is that attention span we discussed earlier. If an audience is overloaded with data, they'll stop listening.

- **Review and Restate:** Explain that this is the part of the presentation where they'll summarize by reviewing and restating the information and flowing straight into the closing. This point in the presentation corresponds to the third step of the popular formula, *Tell them what you're going to tell them, tell them, and then tell them what you told them.* By restating the information in different terms, the speaker can keep from insulting the audience's intelligence or sounding simply repetitive.

- **First Closing:** Ask participants to suggest ideas for a closing and write them on the flipchart. Note that many of the options they might use for an opening, such as quotations and anecdotes, are appropriate choices for closings too.

- **Question-and-Answer Period:** This section will be used for presentations that include a time for questions from the audience. This is where the speaker should consider the topic and the audience, and then list questions that might be asked.

- **Second Closing:** This is a great secret of seasoned presenters. Novice speakers often complete the Q&A segment with a whimper instead of a bang—just sort of drifting off. The impact of even the most inspiring closing statement is lost in that drift. Having a second closing prepared lets the speaker end the Q&A with power. Use the same rules for this closing as for the first closing, and create a statement that reinforces the presentation's purpose one last time.

1:40   Visual Aids (30 minutes)

Show slide 9–18. Most learners are visual learners. For this reason, using visual aids has become a major factor in creating successful presentations. Hand out Tool 12–8 and discuss.

2:10   Challenging Situations (25 minutes)

Show slide 9–19. Distribute Training Instrument 12–13. Follow the instructions in Learning Activity 11–15. This is an opportunity for participants to consider how they would handle distractions and disruptions during their presentations.

2:35   Break (10 minutes)

2:45   Practice Session Preparation (20 minutes)

Show slide 9–20. Distribute Training Instrument 12–14. Conduct Learning Activity 11–16. If you've decided to videotape the presentations, this is the time to get tapes and camera ready.

3:05   Practice Sessions and Feedback (60 minutes)

Show slide 9–21. As participants deliver their presentations, their partners from the introduction exercise at the beginning of the class will prepare feedback for them, using Assessment 12–4.

4:05   Action Plan (10 minutes)

Show slide 9–22 and distribute Training Instrument 12–15. Perform the activity as described in Learning Activity 11–18. Participants will fill out the commitment form and share it with a partner in the class for follow-up.

4:15   Program Evaluation (5 minutes)

Distribute Assessment 12–2. Reinforce the idea of continual development by asking for their input on the evaluation form. When you show your commitment to your own continued skill development, you demonstrate that this should be an ongoing process for them as well.

4:20   Review and Closing (10 minutes)

Ask for questions. Review the sticky-notes posted on the flipchart and in the Parking Lot to be sure that you have covered all the topics they needed you to address. If not, take the time to discuss these topics, answer additional questions, or refer them to the resources for further information.

Use the beach ball that you used in Learning Activity 11–17, tossing it and asking each person to tell one thing he or she has gotten from this workshop.

Finally, using one of your favorite quotes or stories, close the program as you have told them to do—with a great flourish.

What to Do Next

◆ Using the material in chapter 4 as a guide, build a detailed plan to prepare for this workshop.

◆ Schedule a training room and invite your attendees.

◆ Draft a supply list, teaching notes, and time estimates.

◆ Decide how you will support the action plan to which your learners will commit.

◆ Follow each of the steps of your workshop plan to prepare and present your program.

◆ Evaluate the effectiveness of the program, using the ideas from chapter 6.

◆ Consider designing follow-up sessions to encourage the learners to continue developing presentation skills.

Slide 9–1

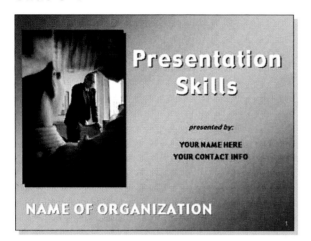

Slide 9–2

Slide 9–3

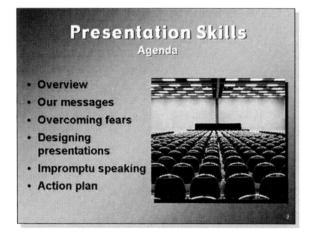

Slide 9–4

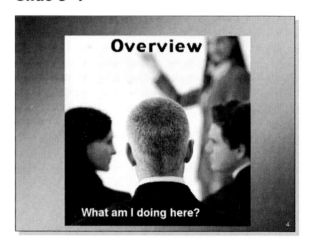

Slide 9–5

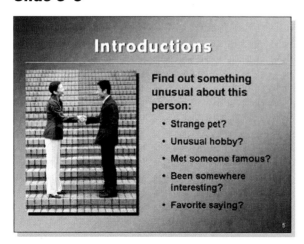

Slide 9–6

Slide 9–7

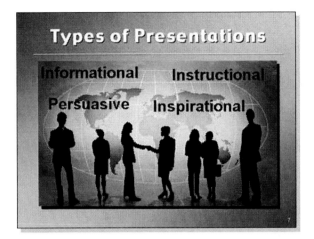

Slide 9–8

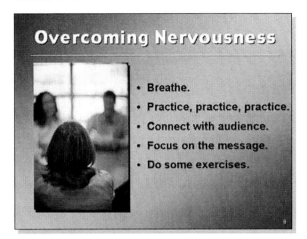

Slide 9–9

Slide 9–10

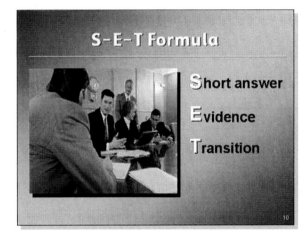

Slide 9–11

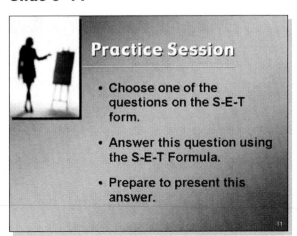

Slide 9–12

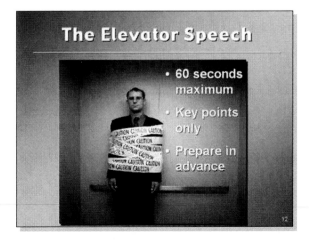

Slide 9–13

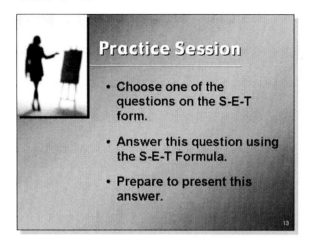

Slide 9–14

Slide 9–15

Slide 9–16

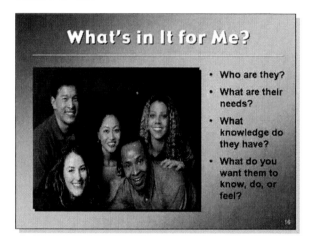

Slide 9–17

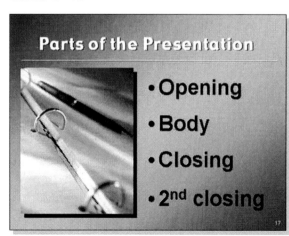

Slide 9–18

Slide 9–19

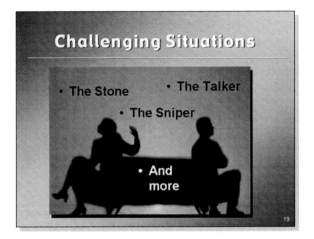

Slide 9–20

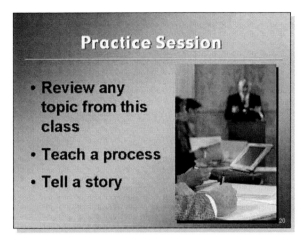

Slide 9–21

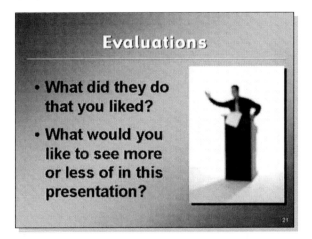

Slide 9–22

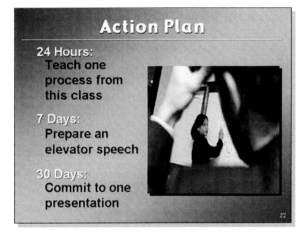

Slide 9–23

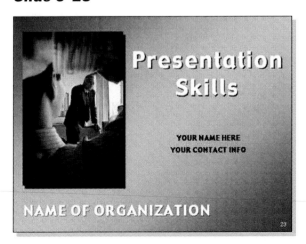

Two-Day Program

- Objectives for the two-day presentation skills workshop

- Lists of materials for facilitator and participants

- Detailed program agenda to be used as a facilitator's guide

The two-day workshop provides time for learners to explore and understand all aspects of the process of planning, designing, and writing effective presentations. The length of this workshop enables participants to deliver various types of presentations so that they build confidence and are able to conclude the program by delivering presentations they've designed. Before leaving the workshop, they will receive feedback from their peers and will create an action plan for continued development.

Training Objectives

The participants' objectives for the two-day presentation skills workshop are to

- design presentations that inform, instruct, persuade, or inspire an audience

- present and facilitate programs in a variety of formats

- adapt presentations to accommodate the needs of different audiences

- use presentation tools and techniques to keep audiences engaged.

Materials

For the facilitator:

- ◆ This chapter for reference and use as a facilitator guide

- ◆ Learning Activity 11–1: Introductions

- ◆ Learning Activity 11–2: Red Flags

- ◆ Learning Activity 11–3: Tone Exercise

- ◆ Learning Activity 11–4: Body Language

- ◆ Learning Activity 11–5: Overcoming Nervousness

- ◆ Learning Activity 11–6: Review

- ◆ Learning Activity 11–7: Brainstorming

- ◆ Learning Activity 11–8: The S-E-T Formula

- ◆ Learning Activity 11–9: S-E-T Practice Session

- ◆ Learning Activity 11–10: Building Rapport

- ◆ Learning Activity 11–11: Writing Your Presentation

- ◆ Learning Activity 11–12: Delivering Your Presentation

- ◆ Learning Activity 11–13: Visual Aids

- ◆ Learning Activity 11–14: Using Microsoft PowerPoint Software

- ◆ Learning Activity 11–15: Challenging Situations

- ◆ Learning Activity 11–16: Presentation Practice Session

- ◆ Learning Activity 11–17: Speaking Opportunities

- ◆ Learning Activity 11–18: Action Plan

- ◆ Tool 12–1: Review Game

- ◆ PowerPoint slide program, titled "Presentation Skills" (slides 10–1 through 10–46). To access slides for this program, open the file *Two-Day.ppt* on the accompanying website. Thumbnail versions of the slides for this two-day workshop are included at the end of this chapter.

◆ Projector, screen, and computer for displaying PowerPoint slides; alternatively, overhead transparencies and overhead projector

◆ *Optional:* Video camera

For the participants:

◆ Copies of all the slides in the PowerPoint presentation, printed three per page; one set of handouts for each learner, three-hole punched and placed in a binder

◆ One flipchart and four markers for each group of four participants

◆ Assorted toys scattered on the tables to help kinesthetic learners occupy their hands and increase their concentration while listening to discussions

◆ Assessment 12–1: Self-Assessment

◆ Assessment 12–2: Program Evaluation

◆ Assessment 12–3: Learning Styles

◆ Assessment 12–4: Presenter Evaluation

◆ Tool 12–2: Presentation Planning Form

◆ Tool 12–3: Pre-Presentation Questionnaire

◆ Tool 12–4: Presentation Checklist

◆ Tool 12–5: On-site Checklist

◆ Tool 12–6: Tips for Delivering Presentations

◆ Tool 12–7: Top Tips for Presentation Gestures and Body Language

◆ Tool 12–8: Guidelines for Visual Aids

◆ Tool 12–9: Flipchart Tips

◆ Tool 12–10: Developing Your Sense of Humor

◆ Tool 12–11: Icebreaker and Energizer Activities

◆ Training Instrument 12–1: Introductions

◆ Training Instrument 12–2: Red Flags

- ◆ Training Instrument 12–3: Tone

- ◆ Training Instrument 12–4: Body Language

- ◆ Training Instrument 12–5: Overcoming Nervousness

- ◆ Training Instrument 12–6: Guidelines for Preparing a Presentation Planning Form

- ◆ Training Instrument 12–7: Brainstorming

- ◆ Training Instrument 12–8: The S-E-T Formula

- ◆ Training Instrument 12–9: S-E-T Practice

- ◆ Training Instrument 12–10: Presentation Action Plan

- ◆ Training Instrument 12–11: Building Rapport

- ◆ Training Instrument 12–12: Microsoft PowerPoint Guidelines

- ◆ Training Instrument 12–13: Challenging Situations

- ◆ Training Instrument 12–14: Practice Session Planning Form

- ◆ Training Instrument 12–15: Continued Development Action Plan

- ◆ *Optional:* assorted snacks or candies (some sugar-free) in cups

- ◆ *Optional:* one blank videotape for each participant

DOWNLOADS

Using the Website

Materials for the training session are provided in this workbook and as electronic files on the accompanying website. To access the electronic files, go to the website and click on the appropriate Adobe .pdf document. Further directions and help using the files can be found in the appendix titled "Using the Website" at the back of this workbook.

It's important that you review all of the slides as part of your preparation for the workshop. As you review them, plan explanations and examples for concepts presented in the slides.

Workshop Preparation

Before the class begins, set the room with the following items:

- flipchart titled "What I Need From Today's Session Is ... "

- PowerPoint slide 10–1

- posted agenda for the day, which includes the lunch break

- binder with participants' handouts at each seat

- sticky-notes attached to each binder

- pencils or pens

- blank paper for each participant

- name badge for each participant

- assorted snacks and candies, as desired.

Sample Agenda

The times assigned to the elements of this training are approximate and will vary with discussion and facilitator emphasis.

FIRST DAY

8:00 a.m.   Welcome (10 minutes)

As participants enter the room, welcome them and ask them to write on a sticky-note one thing that they'd like to get from this workshop on presentation skills. When they've written their notes, instruct them to go up and affix them to the flipchart page displayed at the front of the room.

Introduce yourself and the purpose of the workshop. Go over the ground rules for the session. Here are some sample ground rules and housekeeping items:

- Turn cell phones to silent.

- Because this workshop is interactive, be prepared to participate!

- There will be scheduled breaks in the morning and afternoon.

- Lunch break will be one hour.

- Restrooms, smoking areas, snacks, and vending machines are located in the following areas: *[add details]*.

- Respectful communication is required. If someone is speaking, all attention should be given to that person.

If participants don't know the area, it's a good idea to have maps to nearby restaurants or menus they can use to order lunch.

8:10   Objectives (5 minutes)

Show slide 10–2. Review the workshop objectives.

8:15   Agenda (5 minutes)

Show slide 10–3. Go through the agenda items and ask for any questions.

8:20   Participant Goals (10 minutes)

Show slide 10–4. Read the sticky-notes from the flipchart and assure attendees that the program will address those topics. If any of the topics listed won't be brought up, you can add them to the question-and-answer (Q&A) period at the end of the workshop.

8:30   Introductions (20 minutes)

Show slide 10–5. Distribute Training Instrument 12–1. Perform Learning Activity 11–1. These introductions and the discussion set the stage for the following assessment of presentation skills comfort levels.

8:50   Self-Assessments (25 minutes)

Show slide 10–6. Distribute Assessment 12–1. Ask learners to complete this assessment individually. Assure them that the answers they give are for their eyes only, so they can be completely candid.

When everyone is finished, briefly discuss the questions on the assessment. Ask if they discovered areas that they would like to develop. Ask if they are more comfortable with planned speaking or with impromptu speaking. Did they find that their biggest challenge is writing presentations or presenting them? Discuss how today's workshop will help in each of those areas.

On slide 10–6, click the mouse to reveal each type of presenter as you discuss it.

- **Avoiders:** those who avoid speaking at all

- **Resisters:** those who resist speaking, but can do it if forced

- **Reluctants:** those who don't mind speaking, but don't seek out opportunities

- **Enthusiasts:** those who actively seek opportunities to speak.

After you've explained all four groups, use the following lighthearted approach to identify the comfort level of individual attendees. Doing this ensures that no one is embarrassed and gives you an opportunity to see which participants might need extra encouragement.

Explain that this is an "informal" assessment of each person's presenter type. Ask for a show of hands in response to these questions:

1. Who would rather have a root canal than be asked to give a speech? You're our *avoiders*.

2. Who would prefer to be sitting in the back of the room enjoying the presentation, but could speak if absolutely necessary? You're our *resisters*.

3. Who really doesn't mind speaking in front of a group, but can think of a lot of things you'd rather do? You're our *reluctants*.

4. Who lives for captive audiences? Who wants to turn around to others in the elevator and say, "I suppose you wonder why I've called this meeting"? You are our *enthusiasts*.

9:15   Types of Presentations (15 minutes)

Show slide 10–7. Remind them that, just as there are different types of speakers, there are different types of presentations.

Tell learners to call out reasons they are asked to give speeches and presentations. Write these reasons on a flip-chart page. (If you have an attendee who looks anxious to get involved, ask that person to be your scribe and to do the writing for you.) If necessary, start with your own examples, such as reporting on project progress in staff meetings and explaining new procedures in the office.

Explain the four types of presentations listed on slide 10–7. Click to reveal each type as you discuss it:

◆ **Informational:** This is one type of presentation we do quite often. Its purpose is to give information to the group—a project update, a new employee orientation, or a book report.

◆ **Instructional:** This is an easy one. Ask attendees where they are today. Workshops and training classes are examples of instructional presentations. These presentations teach and demonstrate how to do processes.

◆ **Persuasive:** This type of presentation seeks to initiate action and can include anything from a political candidate's speech to a talk about home security systems to a neighborhood watch committee. Its purpose is to influence the audience to adopt a particular point of view or take some action.

◆ **Inspirational:** This type of presentation seeks to create certain feelings in the audience, to motivate or lift the spirits of the audience. Religious, motivational, and even some purely entertaining speeches can be inspirational.

When you've completed the discussion of presentation types, ask participants to help you link the type of presentation to each example written on the flipchart. Underline each type in a different color.

9:30   Break (15 minutes)

9:45   ABCs of Presentations (10 minutes)

Show slide 10–8. There are three main laws of presentations that should be kept in mind. Click on the slide to reveal each law as you discuss it.

◆ **Accurate:** Any facts, quotations, or statistics we give in our presentations should be checked for validity. When a presenter uses a quote, he or she should tell who said it. If a presentation includes specific statistics or startling facts, the presenter should name the source of that information. If not referenced during the talk, the information can be included in the handouts that accompany the presentation. Doing so ensures accuracy and adds to the credibility of the presentation.

◆ **Brief:** There are lots of studies that argue the length of the average adult's attention span. Twenty minutes is often cited, but it depends on many factors, including environmental conditions, cultural differences, the material's degree of difficulty, and the listener's interest in the topic. Some surveys have suggested that the average adult "checks out" about once every 8 minutes. (This is a fun opportunity to throw out the question, "Is anybody checked out right now?" You don't have to wait for an answer before you reassure them, "Don't worry—you're normal!") The general consensus that our attention spans are getting shorter is a good reason to keep presentations brief.

◆ **Clear:** Ask if any participant has been in a presentation where the speaker used unfamiliar terms and acronyms. Ask how this experience felt. Remind them that using language the audience doesn't understand is a waste of time for everyone. That's why it's beneficial to practice presentations with someone who doesn't understand the topic. That gives the presenter an opportunity to discover which concepts and terms might confuse the audience.

9:55   The Parts of Our Messages (10 minutes)

Show slide 10–9. Ask, "What are the parts of the messages that people send?" The answers you'll get are *words, tone,* and *body language.* Ask learners to guess which part is the least important. It's words. Click on the slide to reveal each message part as you discuss it.

It was psychologist Albert Mehrabian who originally came up with the formula showing that an audience's total "liking" of a message (their positive response to it) was made up of 7 percent verbal (words), 38 percent vocal (tone), and 55 percent facial (body language) components. With time, this hypothesis has been generalized and somewhat misrepresented, but the basic concept is that the smallest effect of our spoken messages comes from the actual words we say.

Tone is the next most important part of a message. And the most important part of the message we send is the facial expression and body language that accompanies it.

Knowing the impact of the three message parts gives us a good guideline to follow. If words are the smallest part of the messages we send, it's definitely worthwhile to consider tone and body language when we're giving a presentation.

You can illustrate this conflict to the group by modeling conflicting presentation behavior. Stand in front of one person in the room, cross your arms tightly, look angrily at that person, and use a harsh tone as you say, "I'm open to any suggestions you have."

Ask if anyone in the room believes you. Ask why they don't. When they mention your tone and body language, agree that those were in conflict with the words you were saying, and that the words were given the least importance. Remind them that we often send conflicting messages like this. This conflict can be confusing for an audience, and it's something speakers need to be aware of when they make presentations.

Tell participants that the group now will look at each part of the message separately and practice techniques to ensure that all the components of their presentations are sending the same message.

10:05   Red Flags (20 minutes)

Show slide 10–10. Distribute Training Instrument 12–2. Perform the activity as described in Learning Activity 11–2. This activity can be expanded or condensed depending on the number of suggestions you take from the participants. For groups that need more time to become comfortable with discussion, this can serve as a non-intimidating approach to encourage them to speak out in class. It also can help dispel nervousness because some unexpected red flags can be quite entertaining.

10:25   Tone (20 minutes)

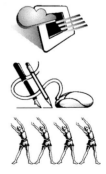

Explain that now that you've discussed the words of their presentations, you'd like to move on to the next-most-influential part of a message. Ask if anyone recalls what that was. When they respond, "the tone," show slide 10–11. Distribute Training Instrument 12–3. Perform the activity as described in Learning Activity 11–3.

10:45   Body Language (20 minutes)

Ask what the most influential part of a message is. When learners respond, "body language," show slide 10–12.

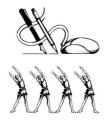

Remind them that facial expression is a major component of our message—but not the only aspect of body language. Point out the other items listed on this slide—eye contact, gesture, posture, and movement. Distribute Training Instrument 12–4. Perform the activity as described in Learning Activity 11–4.

11:05   Overcoming Nervousness (30 minutes)

Show slide 10–13. Lead into this discussion by noting that talking about the body language part of a message brings you to the specific body language of knocking knees, shaking hands, and sweaty palms. Ask what these signs indicate.

These physical responses are some of the signs of fear. Remind learners that anyone who experiences these responses is not alone. We've all heard of the survey that found public speaking to be Americans' number-one fear. Even seasoned speakers may grow anxious when preparing to stand in front of a group. This anxiety shows they still care about getting their messages across to the audience. That concern is a good thing!

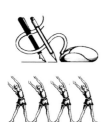

So how do they conquer that fear? Explain that learners' best ideas for handling any stressful situations can be useful for presentation anxiety. Pass out copies of Training Instrument 12–5. Perform the activity as described in Learning Activity 11–5.

Follow up with any items on slide 10–13 that were not covered by the group.

Click on slide 10–13 to show these examples:

◆   **Breathe:** Invite participants to take a deep breath. Hold it to a count of four. Then release the breath, counting slowly from eight down to one. Slowing the breathing like this replicates calm breathing and can help trick the mind into a more relaxed disposition.

◆ **Practice, practice, practice:** We've all heard the answer to the question, How do I get to Carnegie Hall? "Practice, practice, practice." Remind learners that this is great advice, whether they're trying to overcome fear or to present better speeches. It's also the way they'll nip those negative habits like the irritating "uhs" that punctuate sentences or the jingling of coins in a pocket. Suggest that they practice a presentation until they're sure they have it right. Then practice some more.

◆ **Connect with audience:** Ask learners if they felt more comfortable talking to their groups in this exercise than they did in the first exercise of the day. Explain that connecting with their listeners can help them when they're speaking to an audience. Suggest that they learn about the audience before the day of the presentation, and that they arrive early to visit with audience members before the presentation. It's easier to talk to a group when there are some familiar faces in the audience.

It's also possible to establish connections with listeners *during* presentations. A speaker can ask the audience questions, connect with eye contact, and use icebreaker exercises or ask people to introduce themselves. Any of these actions can help lower a speaker's level of nervousness.

◆ **Focus on the message:** Concentrating on the message that one is trying to get across—instead of on one's appearance and on what the audience is thinking—is a great way to relieve the pressure of speaking. As the presenter stands to speak, she or he should hold a quick internal pep rally to highlight the reasons why it's important to get this point across. Focusing on the main theme of the message and how it will benefit the listeners not only helps build confidence, but also boosts the speaker's enthusiasm level.

◆ **Perform practice exercises:** Try a visualization exercise. Some people take a photo of the room where they're going to present their program so they can practice with the photo in front of them. When they get into the room, it's like they've practiced there dozens of times before. Spending a few minutes alone, meditating or practicing breathing and visualizing a successful presentation, can do wonders to counteract the jitters.

To illustrate additional ideas for this calming process, ask the class to try this simple exercise for nerves: Have them put their hands down and grip each side of their chair seats. Tell them to tighten every muscle, hold them tense for 8 seconds, then release. Ask if they feel the difference. Doing this immediately before standing up to deliver a presentation can help relieve tension.

Vocal exercises are also excellent preparation if speakers have a private area available to them. They can repeat some of the standard tongue-twister phrases like "rubber baby buggy bumper" or do face stretches to get loosened up.

Bring the morning session to a close by noting that you've worked on the way speakers present messages, and that, after lunch, you'll shift the focus to developing the content of a presentation.

11:35   Lunch Break (60 minutes)

12:35 p.m.   Review of Topics Covered (15 minutes)

Conduct Learning Activity 11–6.

12:50   Constructing the Presentation (60 minutes)

Show slide 10–14. Pass out Training Instrument 12–6. Explain that creating presentations is as simple as *Get Ready, Get Set, Go:*

- **Get Ready** stands for the planning phase of presentation design. This includes the brainstorming and research stages of a presentation.

- **Get Set** is the next phase. It consists of organizing the information gathered into a cohesive whole, using the *S-E-T formula* (which we'll cover a little later).

- **Go** is the actual writing phase of presentation design.

Refer participants to Training Instrument 12–6, instructing them to use this to make notes about the steps of preparation. Distribute Tool 12–2 and explain that this is a blank form they can keep, copy, and use whenever they need to plan a presentation.

Describe how to complete each of the following blanks on the Presentation Planning Form:

- **Topic:** List your basic topic of discussion.

- **Date:** Insert the date of the presentation.

- **Time:** Note the time your presentation will begin and end.

- **Event/Theme:** Indicate if this presentation is part of a larger event. Define the overall theme of that event.

- **Attendees:** Write the number of people expected.

- **Location:** Insert the exact address and room number for your presentation.

- **Room Setup:** Describe how the chairs and tables will be arranged. Briefly explain the advantages and considerations of the various seating arrangements and remind them to make notes on the form.

  Auditorium seating works well for informational meetings, progress reports, or other presentations where the audience will mainly receive information with minimal interaction. It can also accommodate the largest number of participants in the smallest amount of space.

Classroom seating can be used for sessions where the facilitator will be addressing the group for a major portion of the session and where the participants will need table space to take notes and interact in smaller groups.

U-shape seating is optimal for full group inter-action and allows the facilitator to easily speak to participants individually during the session.

Banquet seating works well for meetings that include meals, but it is best if seating is in a cres-cent formation, which means that seating is only on the sides of the table that can see the speaker without having to completely turn around in their seats.

♦ **Purpose:** Show slide 10–15 and explain that the purpose of a presentation is the ultimate reason for which you're making the presentation—that is, es-sentially ensuring that the audience knows some-thing, does something, or feels something when the presentation is over. Ask if participants remem-ber the four types of presentations you discussed earlier. The type broadly identifies the purpose: Informational and instructional presentations help the listener know or do something; persuasive pre-sentations encourage the listener to take an action; inspirational presentations are meant to prompt feelings in the listener. No matter which goal a speaker has in mind, here's a good rule of thumb: if you can't state the purpose of the presentation in a single sentence, you haven't defined the topic well enough.

Ask participants to try stating the purpose of to-day's workshop in one sentence. Let them come up with their own purpose statements for the class. All their statements will be valid because they present what the individual listener needs and hopes to get from the class.

◆ **Audience Notes:** Show slide 10–16, and distribute Tool 12–3. An analysis of the anticipated audience is the part of the preparation process that directs speakers to find out about the group they'll be addressing.

Ask participants what things they'd like to know about their audiences. Write their answers on a flipchart page. Sample answers might include the average age of the attendees, their average educational level, whether the group will be hostile to the idea being presented, whether listeners are expecting to be entertained or to be informed, and what the audience already knows about the topic. These are the things speakers want to know so they can be sure to include a good dose of *what's in it for me?* in the introduction. The audience members need to understand what they're going to gain from listening; otherwise, they won't be engaged in the presentation.

To help your participants see how making notes about the audience helps them craft a presentation, first give them these specifics: *You are giving a presentation on time management to a group of 25-year-olds who don't think that time management is important to them.* Next, ask them for examples of how this audience profile would affect the way they present the information.

1:50   Brainstorming (20 minutes)

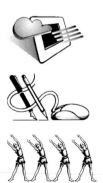

Show slide 10–17. The next segment of the Presentation Planning Form that your participants will work on is the section covering the **Main Points** of the presentation. This is where brainstorming is useful. Distribute Training Instrument 12–7. Perform the activity as described in Learning Activity 11–7.

2:10

Parts of the Presentation (20 minutes)

Continuing with the sections of the Presentation Planning Form, discuss the remaining portions:

- **Opening:** Show slide 10–18. Ask the group to suggest ideas for openings and write them on the flipchart. Examples of good openings include rhetorical questions, startling statistics, quotations, anecdotes, surveys, and humor. Discuss some of your favorite sources for opening materials, including current websites.

- **Point One, Point Two, and Point Three:** Using three main points is a good standard to start with because surveys have shown that listeners tend to be able to retain that number of points. Of course, whether a three-point structure will work for your audience depends on the topic. The most important thing to keep in mind is that attention span we discussed earlier. If an audience is overloaded with data, they'll stop listening.

- **Review and Restate:** Explain that this is the part of the presentation where they'll summarize by reviewing and restating the information and flowing straight into the closing. This point in the presentation corresponds to the third step of the popular formula, *Tell them what you're going to tell them, tell them, and then tell them what you told them.* By restating the information in different terms, the speaker can keep from insulting the audience's intelligence or sounding simply repetitive.

- **First Closing:** Ask participants to suggest ideas for a closing and write them on the flipchart. Note that many of the options they might use for an opening, such as quotations and anecdotes, are appropriate choices for closings too.

- **Question-and-Answer Period:** This section will be used for presentations that include a time for questions from the audience. This is where the speaker should consider the topic and the audience, and then list questions that might be asked.

- ◆ **Second Closing:** This is a great secret of seasoned presenters. Novice speakers often complete the Q&A segment with a whimper instead of a bang—just sort of drifting off. The impact of even the most inspiring closing statement is lost in that drift. Having a second closing prepared lets the speaker end the Q&A with power. Use the same rules for this closing as for the first closing, and create a statement that reinforces the presentation's purpose one last time.

2:30   Break (10 minutes)

2:40   Impromptu Speaking (20 minutes)

Show slide 10–19. Ask for examples of times when participants are called on to do impromptu speaking and what types of topics they're asked to address.

Show slide 10–20. The S-E-T Formula is a simple method for speakers to organize their thoughts when they're asked to make an impromptu presentation. Here are the three factors in the formula:

- ◆ **S = short answer.** Give the bottom-line answer first.

- ◆ **E = evidence supporting the answer.** Elaborate a little by giving the evidence and why it supports the short answer.

- ◆ **T = transition.** Here the speaker summarizes and transitions to the next point or person.

Distribute Training Instrument 12–8. Perform the activity as described in Learning Activity 11–8.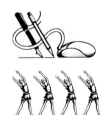

The S-E-T Formula also can be used to construct each section of a longer presentation. It's a formula that keeps the speaker focused as she or he explains or addresses each point in a talk. The "elevator speech" uses this formula.

3:00   Elevator Speech (10 minutes)

Show slide 10–21. Explain that elevator speeches are based on this idea: What if there were someone you've been trying to meet with and you find yourself on the elevator with that person? You have only a few floors to get an idea across to this person. An elevator speech can fulfill that need. It's a brief talk on a subject that's important to the speaker. It should last no more than 30 seconds so it actually can be told in the span of an elevator ride, and it should include the basic points that are important for the listener to know about the topic.

Remind participants that it's an excellent idea to rehearse elevator speeches on all of their current projects. Then, when they find themselves in situations where they need to present this information briefly and concisely, they're ready to make the most of the opportunity.

Here's an example of an instant project update using the S-E-T formula: Your manager asks, "How's that ABC project going?" You answer

- ◆ **S:** *It's right on schedule.*

- ◆ **E:** *We've completed phases 1 and 2 and we'll start phase 3 on Monday. We anticipate having the draft of the project on your desk at the end of next week.*

- ◆ **T:** *Does that work for you?*

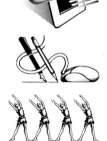

3:10   S-E-T Practice Session (75 minutes)

Show slide 10–22 and distribute Training Instrument 12–9. Explain that learners are going to get a chance to practice an impromptu presentation using the S-E-T Formula. Perform the activity as described in Learning Activity 11–9.

4:25   Action Plan (10 minutes)

Show slide 10–23 and distribute Training Instrument 12–10. Explain that, at the next session, they'll have an opportunity to do a 5-minute presentation on one of the topics suggested on the training instrument.

4:35   Program Evaluation (5 minutes)

Distribute Assessment 12–2. Ask for everyone's suggestions on how the class could be made more effective for them. Let them see that you're open to improvement. Modeling that openness will help them realize that they need to be willing to accept suggestions also.

4:40   Close (10 minutes)

Ask for questions. Solicit volunteers to tell anything they've picked up in today's session that they can use immediately. Remind them of the specifics of the next session. Leave them with a parting joke, quote, or inspirational comment.

SECOND DAY

8:00 a.m.   Welcome and Review of the First Day (10 minutes)

As participants enter the training room, have slide 10–24 showing on the screen. When they're seated, show slide 10–25 and run through the day's agenda. Have a copy of this agenda posted on a flipchart page where everyone can see it throughout the day.

Start this second session with an informal review of items from the first session. Ask participants what they remember from that session. Ask if they have had a chance to use the S-E-T Formula on the job.

8:10   Building Rapport (25 minutes)

Show slide 10–26. Remind learners that getting to know their audience will help boost their comfort level and will improve how well they connect with the group. Visiting with their listeners also helps them gauge the audience's feelings toward the topic. Although many people think that it's impossible to get to know anything about someone in a very short time, the following exercise shows that's not necessarily true.

Distribute Training Instrument 12–11. Perform Learning Activity 11–10.

Ask what members of your class think the slide means by the phrase *observing and adjusting.* If they noticed that audience members looked confused, how could they address the confusion? Stopping to ask for questions at a time like this is an example of observing and adjusting. Do audience members in the back look like they're straining to hear? Perhaps more volume is needed. Ask for other examples of how a presenter might observe and adjust on the spot.

8:35   Writing Your Presentation (15 minutes)

Show slide 10–27. Refer to Training Instrument 12–6. Perform the activity as described in Learning Activity 11–11.

8:50   Delivering Your Presentation: Advance Preparation (20 minutes)

Show slide 10–28. Distribute Tool 12–4. Discuss the items on the Presentation Checklist, asking for learners' input and sharing any personal experiences that reinforce why these preparations are necessary.

9:10   The Day of the Presentation (20 minutes)

Show slide 10–29 and distribute Tool 12–5. Go through the items of the On-site Checklist, asking for input and sharing any personal experiences.

9:30   Break (15 minutes)

9:45   Delivering Your Presentation (35 minutes)

Show slide 10–30. Distribute Tool 12–6. Perform Learning Activity 11–12.

10:20   Gestures (20 minutes)

Show slide 10–31. Hand out Tool 12–7. Discuss the items on this tool and ask participants to suggest additional ways to use gestures and body language effectively.

10:40   Your Audience (15 minutes)

Show slide 10–32. Understanding ourselves as audience members is an excellent way to help us understand our audiences better. This is the fundamental concept that sets the stage for the next assessment. Distribute Assessment 12–3 and ask learners to complete it individually.

10:55   Learning Styles (25 minutes)

Show slide 10–33. As you discuss the results of the learners' self-assessment, click on the slide to reveal the three kinds of learners. Ask participants to suggest ways they can make their presentations appeal to different kinds of learners.

- ◆ **Visual learners:** Handouts, PowerPoint programs, flipcharts, props, videos

- ◆ **Auditory learners:** Discussions, audiovisual presentations, music

- ◆ **Tactile and kinesthetic learners:** Role play, exercises, demonstrations, hands-on practice

11:20   Visual Aids (20 minutes)

Show slide 10–34. Most learners are visual learners. For this reason, using visual aids has become a major factor in creating successful presentations. Hand out Tool 12–8

and conduct Learning Activity 11–13. The groups will practice their presentations before lunch and present them when they return from the lunch break.

11:40　　　Lunch (60 minutes)

12:40 p.m.　Visual Aids Presentations (30 minutes)

1:10　　　Flipcharts (15 minutes)

Show slide 10–35. Hand out Tool 12–9. Invite a volunteer artist from the class to help you by demonstrating as you present key points.

1:25　　　Using PowerPoint Software (20 minutes)

Show slide 10–36. Distribute Training Instrument 12–12 and conduct Learning Activity 11–14.

1:45　　　Challenging Situations (25 minutes)

Show slide 10–37. Distribute Training Instrument 12–13. Follow the instructions in Learning Activity 11–15. This is an opportunity for participants to consider how they would handle distractions and disruptions during their presentations.

2:10　　　Break (10 minutes)

2:20　　　Using Humor (10 minutes)

Show slide 10–38. Distribute Tool 12–10. Ask for suggestions to complete the sayings on the tool. Use the guidelines on this tool to discuss the uses of humor in a presentation and to warn your learners about the wrong types and misuses of humor. Use personal experiences and recent news reports for timely examples.

2:30 Q&A Sessions (10 minutes)

Show slide 10–39. The most effective way to prepare for a Q&A session is to think from the audience's perspective. Speakers preparing for a presentation that includes a Q&A session should make a list of questions the audience might ask and then practice their answers. This also can help expose any parts of a presentation that need to be explained more completely.

Point out another benefit of this kind of preparation: If no one in the audience asks a question, it can create an awkward silence. Speakers who've prepared can simply jump in and ask one of their own questions, with a preface such as, "I'm often asked . . . ," "In case you were wondering about . . . ," or "Here's one point you might have concerns about . . . ."

Reassure participants that it's okay to say, "I don't know." They're not expected to know everything. They can simply offer to find out or, if someone in the group might know the answer, they can open the question for discussion by asking the audience.

Explain that it's always a good practice to restate any questions. This helps ensure the speaker understood the question and that the rest of the audience heard it, and it gives the presenter added time to formulate an answer.

2:40 Practice Session Preparation (20 minutes)

Show slide 10–40. Distribute Training Instrument 12–14. Conduct Learning Activity 11–16. If you've decided to videotape the presentations, this is the time to get tapes and camera ready.

3:00   Practice Sessions and Feedback (60 minutes)

Show slide 10–41. As participants deliver their presentations, the rest of the class will prepare feedback by using Assessment 12–4.

4:00   Activities (10 minutes)

Show slide 10–42. Hand out Tool 12–11. This is a starter list of icebreakers and energizers for meetings or programs. Ask participants why they might want to use an activity in their presentations.

Remind them that there's a reason television sound bites are no more than 30 seconds. For many of us, that's our maximum attention span. That's why presenters often use activities or interactive segments in longer presentations.

Here's another statistic that supports the use of activities: People remember 10 percent of what they hear, 75 percent of what they say, and 90 percent of what they do.

Icebreakers enable people in the room to get to know each other. At many events, some of the best information comes from the people sitting next to us. That's why having opportunities for mini-presentations or networking among audience members can make such a positive addition to their presentations. This is a good time to point out to your participants that, if it's later in the day, an energizer activity can be a great tool for getting participants up and moving around. Use this comment as an introduction to the next segments by telling them you're going to use an energizer activity right now.

4:10   Speaking Opportunities (10 minutes)

Show slide 10–43. Conduct Learning Activity 11–17.

Click on slide 10–43 again to reveal additional suggestions.

4:20   Continued Development (5 minutes)

Show slide 10–44. Discuss the use of mentors, partners, and peers to help your learners continue developing their presentation skills. This section also may include the benefits of recording their presentations for later review.

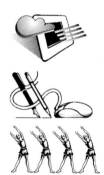

4:25   Action Plan (10 minutes)

Show slide 10–45 and distribute Training Instrument 12–15. Perform Learning Activity 11–18. Participants will fill out the commitment form and share it with a partner in the class for follow-up.

4:35   Program Evaluation (5 minutes)

Distribute Assessment 12–2. Reinforce the idea of continual development by asking for their input on the evaluation form. When you show your commitment to your own continued skill development, you demonstrate that this should be an ongoing process for them as well.

4:40   Review and Closing (10 minutes)

Ask for questions. Review the sticky-notes posted on the flipchart and in the Parking Lot to be sure that you have covered all the topics they needed you to address. If not, take the time to discuss these topics, answer additional questions, or refer them to the resources for further information.

Use the beach ball that you used in Learning Activity 11–17, tossing it and asking each person to tell one thing he or she has gotten from this workshop.

Finally, using one of your favorite quotes or stories, close the program as you have told them to do—with a great flourish.

What to Do Next

◆ Using the material in chapter 4 as a guide, build a detailed plan to prepare for this workshop.

◆ Schedule a training room and invite your attendees.

- Draft a supply list, teaching notes, and time estimates.

- Decide how you will support the action plan to which your learners will commit.

- Follow each of the steps of your workshop plan to prepare and present your program.

- Evaluate the effectiveness of the program, using the ideas from chapter 6.

- Consider designing follow-up sessions to encourage the learners to continue developing presentation skills.

Slide 10–1

Slide 10–2

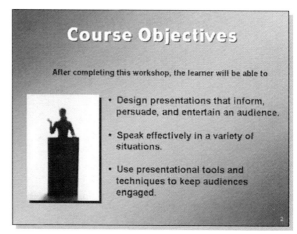

Slide 10–3

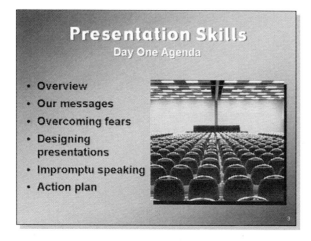

Slide 10–4

Slide 10–5

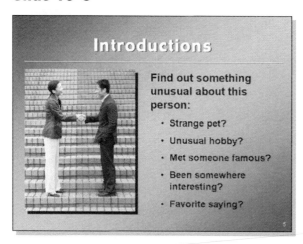

Slide 10–6

Slide 10–7

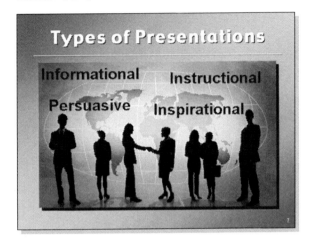

Slide 10–8

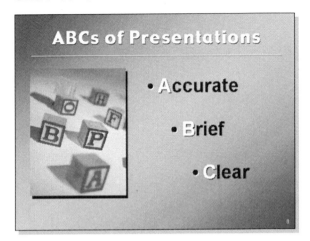

Slide 10–9

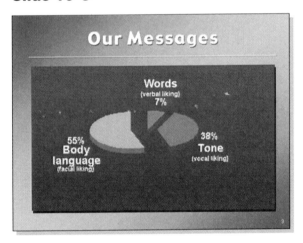

Slide 10–10

Slide 10–11

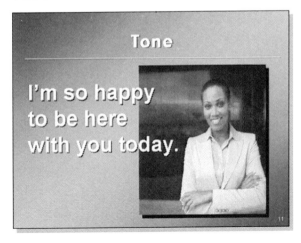

Slide 10–12

Slide 10–13

Overcoming Nervousness

- Breathe.
- Practice, practice, practice.
- Connect with the audience.
- Focus on the message.
- Do some exercises.

Slide 10–14

Constructing Presentations

- Plan
- Design
- Write

Slide 10–15

Purpose

Can you define your purpose for speaking in a single sentence?

Slide 10–16

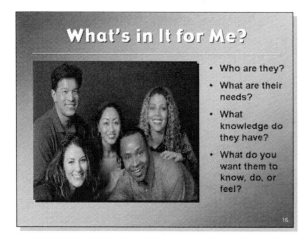

What's in It for Me?

- Who are they?
- What are their needs?
- What knowledge do they have?
- What do you want them to know, do, or feel?

Slide 10–17

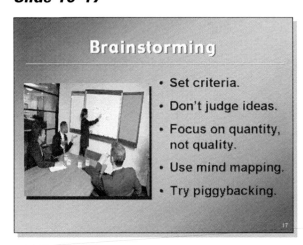

Brainstorming

- Set criteria.
- Don't judge ideas.
- Focus on quantity, not quality.
- Use mind mapping.
- Try piggybacking.

Slide 10–18

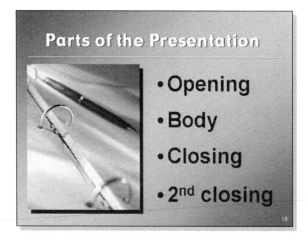

Parts of the Presentation

- Opening
- Body
- Closing
- 2nd closing

Slide 10–19

Slide 10–20

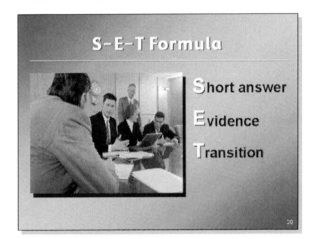

Slide 10–21

Slide 10–22

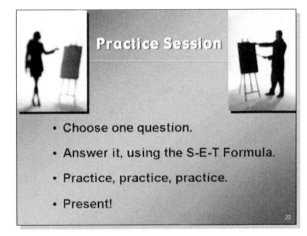

Slide 10–23

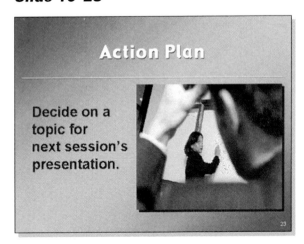

Slide 10–24

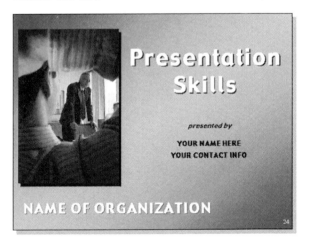

Slide 10–25

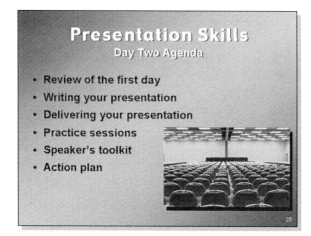

Slide 10–26

Slide 10–27

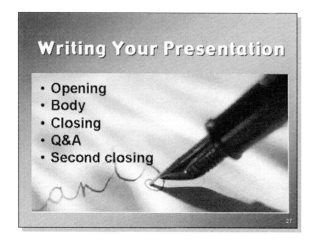

Slide 10–28

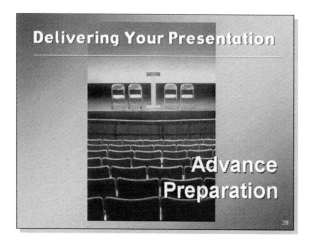

Slide 10–29

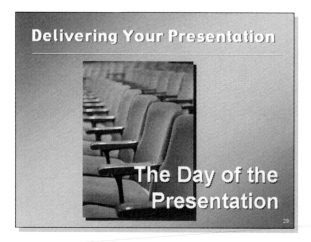

Slide 10–30

Slide 10–31

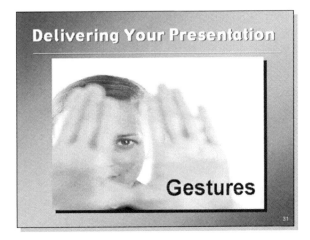

Slide 10–32

Slide 10–33

Slide 10–34

Slide 10–35

Slide 10–36

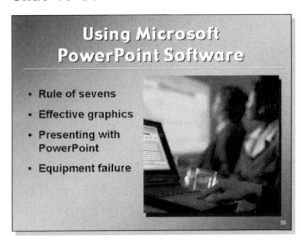

Slide 10–37

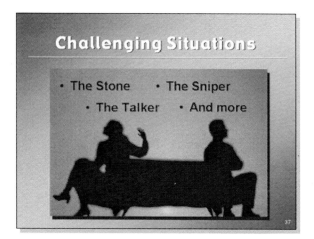

Slide 10–38

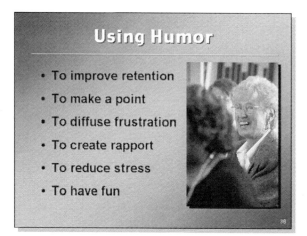

Slide 10–39

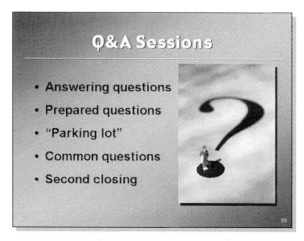

Slide 10–40

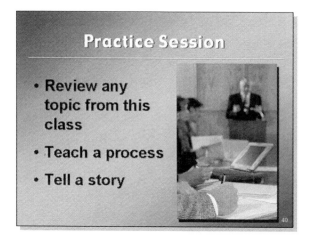

Slide 10–41

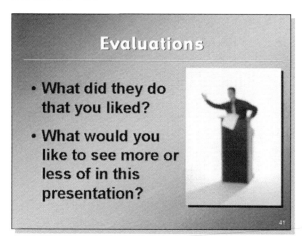

Slide 10–42

Slide 10–43

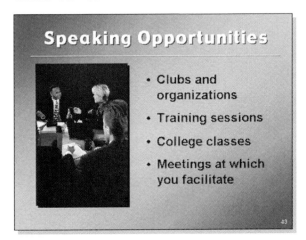

Slide 10–44

Slide 10–45

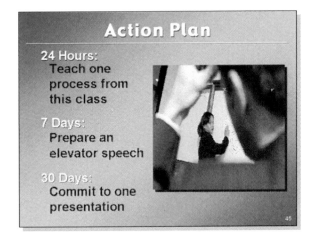

Slide 10–46

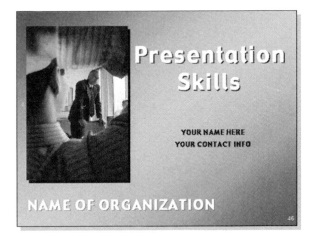

Learning Activities

- Objectives, materials lists, and timeframes for the 18 learning activities used for these workshop formats

- Detailed instructions for conducting each learning activity

This chapter contains the following learning activities used in the various Presentation Skills workshop formats:

- Learning Activity 11–1: Introductions

- Learning Activity 11–2: Red Flags

- Learning Activity 11–3: Tone Exercise

- Learning Activity 11–4: Body Language

- Learning Activity 11–5: Overcoming Nervousness

- Learning Activity 11–6: Review Game

- Learning Activity 11–7: Brainstorming

- Learning Activity 11–8: The S-E-T Formula

- Learning Activity 11–9: S-E-T Practice Session

- Learning Activity 11–10: Building Rapport

- Learning Activity 11–11: Writing Your Presentation

- Learning Activity 11–12: Delivering Your Presentation

- ◆ Learning Activity 11–13: Visual Aids

- ◆ Learning Activity 11–14: Using Microsoft PowerPoint Software

- ◆ Learning Activity 11–15: Challenging Situations

- ◆ Learning Activity 11–16: Presentation Practice Session

- ◆ Learning Activity 11–17: Speaking Opportunities

- ◆ Learning Activity 11–18: Action Plan

Use the chapter in combination with the agenda chapter for your specific workshop format as a facilitator's guide when presenting each session.

Learning Activity 11–1: Introductions

OBJECTIVES

The objectives of this learning activity are to

- ◆ enable participants to get through their first speech quickly

- ◆ help them meet the others who will be their audiences for the later exercises

- ◆ begin increasing their comfort level for later presentations.

MATERIALS

For this activity, you will need

- ◆ Training Instrument 12–1, one copy for each learner

- ◆ pens or pencils for each learner.

TIME

- ◆ 20 minutes

INSTRUCTIONS

1. Hand out copies of Training Instrument 12–1.

2. Instruct participants to find someone they don't know well in the room. If the group is from a department where everyone is acquainted, tell them to find someone they don't work with on a regular basis.

3. Explain that each of them will be introducing their partner to the class. Because they don't want to do a boring introduction, they'll want to discover some unusual facts about that person.

4. Tell them that each of them will have 5 minutes to interview his or her partner. They will use Training Instrument 12–1 to make notes. After 5 minutes, they will switch roles and the other person will become the interviewer. Their goal is to obtain interesting information to use in their introductions. Refer the group to the PowerPoint slide with sample introduction details (slides 7–4, 8–4, 9–5, or 10–5).

5. Start the clock, giving the first interviewer in each pair 5 minutes to gather information.

6. Call time and ask partners to switch roles. Start the clock again and give the new interviewers 5 minutes.

7. Call time. Instruct the group to use Training Instrument 12–1 in keeping notes. During the upcoming introductions, they should write the name of the person being introduced and the interesting fact(s) presented about them.

8. Ask for volunteers to stand with their partners and introduce them to the class. Keep going until all participants have been introduced.

9. Conduct a debriefing discussion, using the following questions.

DISCUSSION QUESTIONS FOR DEBRIEFING

◆ Was this uncomfortable for you?

◆ Was it easier or harder than you thought it would be?

◆ Do you feel more comfortable now that you know a little about the others in the room?

Learning Activity 11–2: Red Flags

OBJECTIVE

The objective of this learning activity is to

- ◆ increase participants' awareness of the language they use and how it can affect the way their messages are received.

MATERIALS

For this activity, you will need

- ◆ Training Instrument 12–2, one copy for each learner

- ◆ one flipchart and easel

- ◆ one red and one blue marker.

TIME

- ◆ 15 minutes

INSTRUCTIONS

1. Hand out copies of Training Instrument 12–2.

2. Ask participants what the phrase *I saw red!* means to them. Explain that seeing red usually means we're angry about something. And that's the concept behind "red-flag statements"—they're statements that make us angry.

3. Draw two columns on the flipchart. Using the red marker, label the first column "Red Flags."

4. Ask class members for examples of a phrase they hate to hear someone say. To prime the pump, start with your examples on slide 10–10.

5. As learners call out their red-flag statements, list them in the Red Flags column. Tell them to write these same statements on Training Instrument 12–2.

6. At the end of the Red Flags list (six to eight entries are enough), add the word *can't*.

7. Now use the blue marker to label the second column on the flipchart "Alternatives." Ask the class members how each statement could be reworded to make it less inflammatory. Click on slide 10–10 to reveal the alternatives for the sample red-flag statements.

8. In the second column of the flipchart, write their suggested alternatives for transforming the red-flag statements in column 1 into more positive messages. When you get to the last one—*can't*—suggest *can* as the alternative. Explain this suggestion with the following example: Red-flag: "I can't do that for you until next week." Positive alternative: "I can do that for you next week" Point out that both statements say exactly the same thing but feel very different.

9. Complete the activity with the following debriefing questions.

DISCUSSION QUESTIONS FOR DEBRIEFING

◆ Have you found yourself using some of these red-flag statements? (Ask them to underline the ones they've used on Training Instrument 12–2 so they can work on eliminating them from their vocabularies.)

◆ What kind of a difference do you think it could make if you removed these types of phrases from your presentations?

◆ Will you commit to not using any red flags in our session today?

Learning Activity 11–3: Tone Exercise

OBJECTIVE

The objective of this learning activity is to

- ◆ increase participants' awareness of how important their tone of voice is to the message they are presenting.

MATERIALS

For this activity, you will need

- ◆ Training Instrument 12–3, one copy for each learner

- ◆ a flipchart and marker

- ◆ pens or pencils for all learners.

TIME

- ◆ 20 minutes

INSTRUCTIONS

1. Hand out copies of Training Instrument 12–3.

2. Show slide 10–11. Explain that this is your practice phrase for today. Ask learners to come up with a phrase they use every day in the workplace. It could be as simple as "Thank you for calling ABC Company." Each person will have her or his own practice phrase. Ask each learner to write his or her phrase in the left column of the training instrument.

3. Ask them to think about the emotions and moods a person might go through at work each day. Do they get frustrated? Do they have silly moments? Do they feel enthusiastic? Do they sometimes even get sarcastic?

4. List these on the flipchart as they call them out. Have them also write them in the right-hand column of the training instrument.

5. Select four of the listed emotions that will be good examples of mood conveyed by tone (for example, enthusiastic, angry, sarcastic, bored), and place checkmarks next to them.

6. Ask volunteers to read their sentences in a tone of voice that reveals each of these emotions. Give them an example to start with by using your practice phrase on slide 10–11.

7. Complete the activity by debriefing with the questions below.

ACTIVITY VARIATIONS

◆ If you have a large group, break them up into smaller groups and have participants read their lines to their groups.

◆ If you have a very large group, ask for a few "thespian" volunteers to come up and act out their lines.

◆ Shorten this exercise by writing on the flipchart, "I didn't say you looked silly today." Then go around the room and have each person emphasize a different word in the sentence to demonstrate how simply changing the emphasis can change the meaning of the sentence.

DISCUSSION QUESTIONS FOR DEBRIEFING

◆ What did you realize from this exercise? (For example, *It's not what you say but how you say it*.) Write this as a reminder on the bottom of the training instrument.

◆ Are there any tones of voice you need to be careful about? (Learners don't have to share this information aloud if they don't want to.) Underline those on the training instrument to remind you to be aware of them.

Learning Activity 11–4: Body Language

OBJECTIVE

The objective of this learning activity is to

- increase participants' awareness of the importance of their body language in the messages they present.

MATERIALS

For this activity, you will need

- Training Instrument 12–4, one copy for each learner

- a flipchart and marker

- pens or pencils for all learners.

TIME

- 15 minutes

INSTRUCTIONS

1. Hand out copies of Training Instrument 12–4.

2. Ask each person to stand and, without any words, get a message across by using body language. (Nothing inappropriate, please!) You can start things out by doing something very obvious like crossing your arms, winking, or giving a thumbs-up.

3. Have the group tell what message it's getting from the body language of each presenter.

4. Write these messages on the flipchart and ask participants to list them on the training instrument.

5. Complete the activity with the following debriefing questions.

DISCUSSION QUESTIONS FOR DEBRIEFING

- What are some of your observations about body language? (This is a good time to note that sometimes we interpret the message differently than what the person thought. That's how mixed signals happen. Sometimes crossed arms indicate a closed-off person, and sometimes the speaker is just chilled.)

♦ What are some other forms of body language we might use without even realizing it? (For example, looking at the clock, tapping fingers, or sighing.)

♦ Freeze. Look around the room right now. What might various people's posture say to someone who was looking in a window?

- ♦ Hand up—wants to talk

- ♦ Leaning back in the seat—bored

- ♦ Head down but not writing—tired

- ♦ Smiling—having fun

- ♦ Talking to the instructor or class—engaged

♦ What lesson should we take from this exercise? Write that lesson as a personal reminder on the bottom of the training instrument.

Learning Activity 11-5: Overcoming Nervousness

OBJECTIVES

The objectives of this learning activity are to

- ◆ let participants discuss nervousness and ways to overcome fear
- ◆ help them continue raising their comfort level by speaking with their classmates.

MATERIALS

For this activity, you will need

- ◆ Training Instrument 12–5, one copy for each learner
- ◆ a flipchart and marker
- ◆ pencils or pens for the learners.

TIME

- ◆ 30 minutes

INSTRUCTIONS

1. Hand out copies of Training Instrument 12–5.

2. Have the participants count off from one to four and gather at tables to form four groups.

3. Give the groups 10 minutes to brainstorm ways to overcome nervousness and stress. Have them list ideas on their training instruments.

4. Give each group 2 minutes to rank their ideas and identify their favorite four methods.

5. Go around the room, asking each team member to stand and present one of the group's four ideas to the class.

6. List a brief description of each of these ideas on the flipchart. Instruct participants to add all of the ideas to their lists on the training instrument.

7. Complete the activity using the debriefing questions below.

DISCUSSION QUESTIONS FOR DEBRIEFING

- Did you think of any other ideas as you were listening to the ones presented by other class members?

- What do you think will be the most useful ideas for you to use in combating nervousness?

Learning Activity 11–6: Review Game

OBJECTIVES

The objectives of this learning activity are to

- ◆ review material that has been discussed thus far in the workshop

- ◆ serve as an energizer by getting participants moving around and interacting.

MATERIALS

For this activity, you will need

- ◆ Tool 12–1.

PREPARATION

Copy Tool 12–1 onto card stock and cut sheets so that you have one card for each question and one card for each answer.

TIME

- ◆ 15 minutes

INSTRUCTIONS

1. Distribute one card to each attendee, making sure that you have distributed the corresponding questions and answers.

2. Instruct each participant to find the person with the question or answer that fits with the card he or she is holding. (If there is an uneven number of participants, hold one of the cards and let the person find you.)

3. When they've all found their partners, have them read their questions and answers aloud and check to ensure that they have made the correct connections.

Learning Activity 11–7: Brainstorming

OBJECTIVE

The objective of this learning activity is to

◆ give participants a chance to practice the basic steps of brainstorming, which will help them create materials for their presentations later in the workshop.

MATERIALS

For this activity, you will need

◆ Training Instrument 12–7, one copy for each learner

◆ a flipchart

◆ markers in multiple colors

◆ pens or pencils for learners.

TIME

◆ 20 minutes

INSTRUCTIONS

1. Hand out copies of Training Instrument 12–7. You have the option of keeping learners in the same groups they formed for Learning Activity 11–6 or having them count off one to four to form new groups.

2. Explain the two main rules of brainstorming:

   a. don't judge ideas

   b. strive for quantity of ideas, not quality.

3. Ask participants to imagine a class on time management skills.

4. Draw a circle in the middle of the flipchart page and label it "Time Management Skills." Instruct learners to write the same label in the circle on their training instruments.

5. Ask them to spend 5 minutes brainstorming in their groups on any topics they'd like covered in a class on time management and then to list them on the training instrument.

6. After 5 minutes, have each group call out their lists and write them on your flipchart.

7. Ask the whole group to help you figure out which topics are parts of similar concepts. Use a different color of marker to circle the words from each related group.

8. Explain that this is the same method they can use to come up with ideas for presentations. In their personal brainstorming sessions, when they've run out of ideas, they should evaluate the ideas and decide which should be combined or deleted from the list, and which can stand alone.

9. Complete the activity with the debriefing questions that follow.

DISCUSSION QUESTIONS FOR DEBRIEFING

◆ Why do you think it's so important not to censor any of your ideas while brainstorming?

◆ There are many formats for brainstorming. Do you use any other methods? Explain.

Learning Activity 11–8: The S-E-T Formula

OBJECTIVE

The objective of this learning activity is to

- ◆ provide practice in relaying clear and concise information with a minimum amount of preparation time.

MATERIALS

For this activity, you will need

- ◆ Training Instrument 12–8, one copy for each learner.

TIME

- ◆ 20 minutes

INSTRUCTIONS

1. Distribute copies of Training Instrument 12–8.

2. Inform the participants that you would like them to practice the S-E-T Formula for communication.

3. Explain that S-E-T comprises the **Short answer,** followed by the **Evidence supporting that answer,** and then a **Transition** made by summarizing the answer and handing the floor back to the questioner (in this situation, you).

4. When each participant chooses one of the questions on the training instrument, she or he will have 10 minutes to prepare an answer, using the S-E-T Formula. The entire answer should be no longer than 60 seconds.

5. When they've completed their answers, each learner will partner with someone in the room and practice delivering the answer.

6. Partners should ask questions if they don't understand the answer so the speaker can revise the answer to make it more understandable.

7. Complete the activity using the debriefing questions below.

DISCUSSION QUESTIONS FOR DEBRIEFING

♦   Did you notice that we often can answer questions in a lot less time than we normally do? Why do you think this is?

♦   How could you use this formula in meetings and other impromptu speaking opportunities?

Learning Activity 11–9: S-E-T Practice Session

OBJECTIVE

The objective of this learning activity is to

- ◆ give participants an opportunity to practice the skills they've learned in today's session in a nonintimidating atmosphere.

MATERIALS

For this activity, you will need

- ◆ Training Instrument 12–9, one copy for each learner
- ◆ pens or pencils for learners.

TIME

- ◆ 75 minutes

INSTRUCTIONS

1. Hand out copies of Training Instrument 12–9.

2. Ask participants to choose one question for their S-E-T presentation.

3. Give them 20 minutes to prepare their talks. Each learner should use up to three pieces of evidence to support his or her answer. The talk should be no longer than 3 minutes.

4. If possible, let participants spread out or move to other rooms to practice alone.

5. Have each participant give her or his presentation.

6. Complete the activity with the debriefing questions that follow.

DISCUSSION QUESTIONS FOR DEBRIEFING

- ◆ How did this presentation feel?
- ◆ Was this easier than your earlier presentations? What do you think made the difference?

Learning Activity 11–10: Building Rapport

OBJECTIVE

The objective of this learning activity is to

♦ demonstrate to participants that it doesn't take a long time to develop rapport or find things in common with other people.

MATERIALS

For this activity, you will need

♦ Training Instrument 12–11, one copy for each learner

♦ pens or pencils for learners.

TIME

♦ 15 minutes

INSTRUCTIONS

1. Hand out copies of Training Instrument 12–11.

2. Ask participants to count off one to four. They will move to sit at a table with the others who have the same number.

3. Each group's mission is to find as many things that all the members have in common as they can identify in 3 minutes.

4. These commonalities can't be as obvious as "We're all in a class." They should be shared experiences such as hobbies, pets, number of children, places traveled, and schools attended.

5. Whenever they find one element they have in common (for example, if everyone has visited Japan), every group member lists the fact on her or his training instrument. If any person in the group doesn't share an item that the rest of the group has in common, it can't be listed.

6. At the end of 3 minutes, see which group identified the most commonalities. Have the groups tell some of the traits they shared.

7. Complete the activity with the following debriefing question.

DISCUSSION QUESTION FOR DEBRIEFING

♦ You were able to come up with this many traits in common in only 3 minutes. How could you adapt this practice to developing rapport with audience members?

Learning Activity 11–11: Writing Your Presentation

OBJECTIVE

The objective of this learning activity is to

◆ have participants practice their impromptu speaking skills by reviewing the Presentation Planning Form, which they will use to write their presentations later in the session.

MATERIALS

For this activity, you will need

◆ Training Instrument 12–6, one copy for each learner

◆ pens or pencils for the learners.

TIME

◆ 15 minutes

INSTRUCTIONS

1. Ask participants to refer to Training Instrument 12–6 that they used to take notes in the previous session. They will use this to make additional notes during the following discussion. Distribute additional copies of the instrument so they can use these clean copies to design their presentations today.

2. Ask for volunteers to stand and explain why each of the items listed on slides 8–11, 9–17, and 10–27 is important. Encourage them to use the S-E-T Formula to answer.

3. Add your comments and clarifications to the explanations, as needed.

4. Conduct a debriefing discussion, using the following questions.

DISCUSSION QUESTIONS FOR DEBRIEFING

◆ Are there any parts of presentation planning covered on the Presentation Planning Form that you haven't considered before?

◆ How do you think considering those areas of planning will improve your presentations?

Learning Activity 11–12: Delivering Your Presentation

OBJECTIVES

The objective of this learning activity are to

- ◆ enable participants to practice various methods of presenting

- ◆ help participants learn skills directly related to the delivery of presentations.

MATERIALS

For this activity, you will need

- ◆ Tool 12–6, one copy for each learner.

TIME

- ◆ 35 minutes

INSTRUCTIONS

1. Distribute Tool 12–6.

2. Divide participants into three groups. Give each group one of the tool's three topics (vocal quality, presentation notes, or facilitation phrases) to teach.

3. Give the groups 10 minutes to determine how they will get this information across to the rest of the class. Perhaps they will choose role-playing, a panel discussion, or even examples of the "wrong and right" ways to present or facilitate. Tell them their presentations may not be longer than 5 minutes.

4. Before having the groups come up to deliver their presentations, take a moment to discuss the idea of respectful communication. Remind them that they should focus all their attention on the group that is presenting and be supportive by not continuing to discuss their upcoming presentations at this time.

5. Call on each group to present their programs.

6. Conduct a debriefing discussion, using the following questions.

DISCUSSION QUESTIONS FOR DEBRIEFING

◆ Which of these tips will be of most use to you?

◆ Do you see how interactions like role playing and panel discussions add energy to a presentation or help illustrate a concept?

◆ Can you think of any examples where you could incorporate interactive activities such as these into your presentations or meetings?

Learning Activity 11–13: Visual Aids

OBJECTIVE

The objective of this learning activity is to

◆ help participants discover the benefits and possible challenges of using different forms of visual aids.

MATERIALS

For this activity, you will need

◆ Tool 12–8, one copy for each learner.

TIME

◆ 20 minutes preparation time

◆ 30 minutes presentation time

INSTRUCTIONS

1. Distribute Tool 12–8.

2. Break the class into five groups by counting off one to five.

3. Assign one visual aid topic (flipcharts, handouts, overhead transparencies, PowerPoint presentations, projection boards) to each group.

4. Explain that each group will create a 5-minute persuasive presentation on the benefits of using its form of visual aid. Groups will have 20 minutes of preparation time. Point out that the rest of the class will be able to ask questions after each presentation and may even debate with them about the benefits claimed for the visual aid. Therefore, each group should prepare for possible questions and should brainstorm ideas for a rebuttal.

5. Tell them that, after lunch, each group will deliver its presentation.

6. When everyone returns from lunch, you'll call on each group to deliver its presentation.

7. After each presentation, encourage the rest of the class to add their ideas of benefits and drawbacks of each form of visual aid. Allow the presenting group to give the final rebuttal.

8. Conduct a debriefing discussion, using the following questions.

DISCUSSION QUESTIONS FOR DEBRIEFING

◆ Had you anticipated any of the audience's potential questions? Which ones? Were you prepared?

◆ How did it make you feel when listeners disagreed with your comments? What would you recommend to others to help them feel more comfortable with handling questions and debate?

Learning Activity 11–14: Using Microsoft PowerPoint Software

OBJECTIVE

The objective of this learning activity is to

- ◆ acquaint attendees with the basics of using PowerPoint for their presentations.

MATERIALS

For this activity, you will need

- ◆ Training Instrument 12–12, one copy for each learner.

TIME

- ◆ 10 minutes

INSTRUCTIONS

1. Distribute Training Instrument 12–12.

2. Ask participants to use the rules on the training instrument to rate the design of the PowerPoint slide on the page.

3. Conduct a debriefing discussion, using the following questions.

DISCUSSION QUESTIONS FOR DEBRIEFING

- ◆ What problems did you find on this slide?

- ◆ What did you like on this slide?

- ◆ What did you discover from this exercise?

- ◆ What resources could be useful in creating PowerPoint presentations?

Learning Activity 11–15: Challenging Situations

OBJECTIVES

The objectives of this learning activity are to

- give all learners an additional opportunity to practice their presentation and facilitation skills

- give learners a chance to formulate ways of handling the challenges that could occur during their presentations.

MATERIALS

For this activity, you will need

- Training Instrument 12–13, one copy for each learner

- a box.

TIME

- 25 minutes

INSTRUCTIONS

1. Distribute the first page of Training Instrument 12–13.

2. Cut page two of the Training Instrument into strips so that you have one challenging behavior on each strip. Place strips in box.

3. Have each attendee pull one challenging behavior strip out of the box and explain how they would handle it. They can use the training instrument for ideas or draw on their own personal experience.

4. Add to the discussion by referring to ideas listed on the training instrument.

5. Conduct a debriefing discussion, using the following questions.

DISCUSSION QUESTIONS FOR DEBRIEFING

- What other kinds of challenges have you experienced during a presentation?

- What recommendations do you have for handling that challenge?

Learning Activity 11–16: Presentation Practice Session

OBJECTIVE

The objective of this learning activity is to

- give participants an opportunity to review and use all the skills they've studied in the workshop.

MATERIALS

For this activity, you will need

- Training Instrument 12–10 from previous session

- one copy of Training Instrument 12–14

- Assessment 12–4, one copy for each learner

- a flipchart and markers

- (optional) one videotape for each participant, a video camera, and tripod.

TIME

- 80 minutes

PREPARATION

1. Post a flipchart page with topic ideas from Training Instrument 12–10.

2. If you are taping presentations, set the video camera on a tripod at the back of the room.

3. Label a videotape for each attendee.

INSTRUCTIONS

1. Refer to the topics from Training Instrument 12–10 that you've posted on the flipchart page.

2. Instruct each participant to choose one topic from that list or to pick any subject that has been covered in class.

3. Everyone is to prepare a 5-minute talk on their chosen topic.

4. They are welcome to use any form of visual aid available in the room.

5. Distribute Assessment 12–4 so everyone can see how they will be evaluated and how they will evaluate others. Discuss the assessment and answer any questions.

6. Give learners 20 minutes of preparation time. It's helpful if you designate nearby areas where they can go so they can practice aloud.

7. When participants reassemble, announce that the person who introduced them at the beginning of the first session will be their evaluator. You also will complete an evaluation on each person.

8. Explain that evaluators are to find things that the person does well and suggest some areas they can work on.

9. (Optional) As each participant gives his or her presentation, videotape it. At the end of the presentation, give the tapes to each person for his or her own private review.

10. Evaluate in the following order:

   a. First, the presenter comments on how the presentation felt. If the speaker has no comments, you can use the discussion questions below to elicit responses.

   b. The evaluator presents his or her notes.

   c. Allow other members of the class to give additional comments.

   d. You give your notes last to ensure that the evaluation ends on a positive note.

11. Conduct a debriefing discussion, using the following questions.

DISCUSSION QUESTIONS FOR DEBRIEFING

   ◆ Did this feel better than your earlier presentations?

   ◆ What do you think you did differently than you would have before you went through this workshop?

   ◆ What part of your presentations skills would you like to continue to develop?

Learning Activity 11-17: Speaking Opportunities

OBJECTIVES

The objectives of this learning activity are to

- ◆ demonstrate the use of activities as an energizer for workshops

- ◆ enable the class to brainstorm opportunities to practice their improved speaking skills.

MATERIALS

For this activity, you will need

- ◆ a beach ball.

TIME

- ◆ 10 minutes

INSTRUCTIONS

1. Ask participants to think of speaking opportunities where they can practice their new and improved speaking skills.

2. You start it off with the beach ball in hand, explaining that you'll throw the ball to someone and she or he should name a speaking opportunity. Then that person will throw the ball to someone else and that person will name another speaking opportunity.

3. The ball should be thrown to each person only one time so all learners have to pay attention to who has already answered. If a learner throws the ball to someone who has had a turn, the ball comes back to the thrower and she or he must give another answer.

4. If anyone has trouble thinking of an answer, the rest of the attendees can help with ideas.

5. Continue playing until all learners have had a turn with the ball.

6. Conduct a debriefing discussion, using the following questions.

DISCUSSION QUESTIONS FOR DEBRIEFING

- ◆ Do you see how an activity like this could help get the energy level up in a room?

- ◆ What other uses could you see for an activity like this?

Learning Activity 11-18: Action Plan

OBJECTIVE

The objective of this learning activity is to

◆ gain the commitment of attendees to continue developing their speaking skills.

MATERIALS

For this activity, you will need

◆ Training Instrument 12–15, one copy for each learner

◆ pens for all learners

◆ one #10 envelope for each learner.

TIME

◆ 10 minutes

INSTRUCTIONS

1. Distribute envelopes and copies of Training Instrument 12–15, and have participants address envelopes to themselves.

2. Instruct them to complete the training instrument, put it in the envelope (without sealing it), and then trade envelopes with someone in the room.

3. Explain that 30 days from this day, each person will mail the envelope to his or her partner as a reminder of the commitment made. Before they mail it, they also will add a bonus item for the partner's file of great openers and closers. This item may be an anecdote, a joke, or some interesting fact.

4. Conduct a debriefing discussion, using the following questions.

DISCUSSION QUESTIONS FOR DEBRIEFING

◆ Did you learn something here that you can use in meetings?

◆ Do any of you have presentations scheduled in the next month?

◆ What will you do differently because of what you've learned here?

Assessments, Tools, and Training Instruments

What's in This Chapter?

- 4 Assessments

- 11 Tools

- 16 Training Instruments

- Instructions for using the electronic versions of these materials that are supplied on the accompanying website

This chapter contains assessments, tools, and training instruments that are used with in the various workshop formats for presentation skills training. Here's a list of the materials in this chapter:

- Assessment 12–1: Self-Assessment

- Assessment 12–2: Program Evaluation

- Assessment 12–3: Learning Styles

- Assessment 12–4: Presenter Evaluation

- Tool 12–1: Review Game

- Tool 12–2: Presentation Planning Form

- Tool 12–3: Pre-Presentation Questionnaire

- Tool 12–4: Presentation Checklist

- Tool 12–5: On-site Checklist

- Tool 12–6: Tips for Delivering Presentations

- Tool 12–7: Top Tips for Presentation Gestures and Body Language

- ◆ Tool 12–8: Guidelines for Visual Aids

- ◆ Tool 12–9: Flipchart Tips

- ◆ Tool 12–10: Developing Your Sense of Humor

- ◆ Tool 12–11: Icebreaker and Energizer Activities

- ◆ Training Instrument 12–1: Introductions

- ◆ Training Instrument 12–2: Red Flags

- ◆ Training Instrument 12–3: Tone

- ◆ Training Instrument 12–4: Body Language

- ◆ Training Instrument 12–5: Overcoming Nervousness

- ◆ Training Instrument 12–6: Guidelines for Preparing a Presentation Planning Form

- ◆ Training Instrument 12–7: Brainstorming

- ◆ Training Instrument 12–8: The S-E-T Formula

- ◆ Training Instrument 12–9: S-E-T Practice

- ◆ Training Instrument 12–10: Presentation Action Plan

- ◆ Training Instrument 12–11: Building Rapport

- ◆ Training Instrument 12–12: Microsoft PowerPoint Guidelines

- ◆ Training Instrument 12–13: Challenging Situations

- ◆ Training Instrument 12–14: Practice Session Planning Form

- ◆ Training Instrument 12–15: Continued Development Action Plan

- ◆ Training Instrument 12–16: Practice Session

Using the Website

The materials in this chapter also appear on the accompanying website. You will find these items by accessing the website and using Adobe Acrobat software to open the .pdf files for the specific materials you wish to use in your training. The files are identified by the number that corresponds to the number in the book. When you locate the files(s) you need, simply print the pages of the document(s) for your session.

Assessment 12–1
Self-Assessment

Instructions: Circle the number on the scale to indicate how often the statement is true. The scale is structured from 5 = Always to 1 = Never.

		ALWAYS				NEVER
1.	I enjoy making presentations and look for opportunities to do so.	5	4	3	2	1
2.	My presentations are well organized and clear.	5	4	3	2	1
3.	I can state the purpose of my presentation in a single sentence.	5	4	3	2	1
4.	I rehearse my presentations repeatedly before delivering them to a group.	5	4	3	2	1
5.	I am comfortable using various forms of visual aids during my presentations.	5	4	3	2	1
6.	I use gestures effectively and comfortably when delivering presentations.	5	4	3	2	1
7.	I anticipate potential questions and practice for Q&A sessions.	5	4	3	2	1
8.	I am comfortable and clear when giving impromptu presentations.	5	4	3	2	1
9.	I maintain a speaker's file of quotations, stories, statistics, and humor to use in presentations.	5	4	3	2	1
10.	I ask audience members to evaluate me when I make presentations.	5	4	3	2	1

Assessment 12–2
Program Evaluation

Name (optional): _____   Company: _____

Course: _____   Instructor: _____

Date: _____   Time: _____

Instructions: Answer the questions below. For questions 1 through 10, circle the appropriate number, using the following scale:

1 = DEFINITELY NO   2 = NO   3 = NOT SURE / NOT APPLICABLE   4 = YES   5 = DEFINITELY YES

1. Did you enjoy this workshop?	5 4 3 2 1
2. Did you obtain the information that you needed?	5 4 3 2 1
3. Will the handouts be valuable as job aids?	5 4 3 2 1
4. Do you feel that the information from this workshop will help improve your presentation skills?	5 4 3 2 1
5. Would you like to attend an advanced course on this topic?	5 4 3 2 1
6. Did the instructor know the subject matter?	5 4 3 2 1
7. Was the pacing of the class comfortable for you?	5 4 3 2 1
8. Were questions answered completely and clearly?	5 4 3 2 1
9. Did the instructor's style of presenting keep your attention and interest in the subject matter?	5 4 3 2 1
10. Would you recommend this program to others?	5 4 3 2 1

11. What would you have liked more of in this program?

12. What would you have liked less of in this program?

13. What is one thing you learned in this program that you will be able to put into practice in the workplace?

Assessment 12-3
Learning Styles

Instructions: To answer the following questions, put a checkmark in the column that represents your preference. Add up your checkmarks in each column and total below.

1. Which of these do you do when you listen to music?	Daydream	Hum along	Move with the music, tap your foot, dance
2. When you work at solving a problem, which of these things do you do?	Make a list, organize the steps, and check them off as they're done	Call or visit with friends or experts to get ideas	Make a model of the problem or walk through all the steps in your mind
3. To learn how a computer works, which of these things would you rather do?	Watch a video	Listen to someone explaining it	Take the computer apart and try to figure it out for yourself
4. Which are you most likely to remember?	Faces but not names	Names but not faces	Events but not details
5. How do you communicate?	Talk quickly, but rarely at length	Enjoy listening, but sometimes can't wait to talk	Find it difficult to listen well; gesture as you speak
6. When you see the word *dog*, what do you do first?	Picture a particular dog	Say the word *dog* to yourself	Sense the feeling of petting or playing with a dog
7. When you tell a story, which of these would you rather do?	Write it	Tell it out loud	Act it out
8. When you're trying to work, which of these are most distracting for you?	Visual distractions	Noises	Other sensations like hunger, tight shoes, or worry
9. When you're trying to learn a new process, which do you prefer?	Reading or watching a demonstration	Listening to a lecture and explanation	Practicing with a hands-on exercise

continued on next page

Assessment 12–3, continued

Learning Styles

	Visual	Auditory	Kinesthetic
10. When you aren't sure how to spell a word, which of these are you most likely to do?	Write it out to see if it looks right	Sound it out	Write it out to see if it feels right
11. Which of these phrases are you more likely to use?	I see what you mean	That sounds right to me	I get the idea
12. Which way do you prefer to conduct meetings?	Face to face	By telephone	In working sessions
13. For recreation, which of these do you prefer?	Watching television	Listening to music	Doing hobbies and crafts
	Column total: _____ **Visual**	*Column total:* _____ **Auditory**	*Column total:* _____ **Kinesthetic**

Assessment 12–4

Presenter Evaluation

Name of presenter_____ **Date** _____

Name of evaluator_____

Instructions: As the presenter performs each of the following actions, place a checkmark in the corresponding box. Make additional notes on areas in which the presenter excels and describe any ideas for areas of development.

PRESENTATION DESIGN	PRESENTATION CONTENT
☐ Gave an introduction that gained attention	☐ Used simple sentences
☐ Stated purpose	☐ Presented information in logical order
☐ Used S-E-T Formula	☐ Used appropriate vocabulary
☐ Closed presentation effectively	☐ Used examples or personal experiences

PRESENTER'S CONNECTION WITH AUDIENCE	PRESENTER'S DELIVERY
☐ Maintained good eye contact	☐ Used a good speed of delivery
☐ Addressed audience needs	☐ Varied the vocal tone
☐ Gave verbal reinforcement	☐ Spoke clearly and at appropriate volume
☐ Involved the audience	☐ Exhibited enthusiasm
☐ Looked for nonverbal clues	☐ Used notes effectively
	☐ Avoided filler words (*uh, um, OK*)

PRESENTER'S BODY LANGUAGE	PRESENTER'S USE OF AUDIOVISUAL AIDS
☐ Maintained a relaxed posture	☐ Used appropriate audiovisuals
☐ Used appropriate gestures	☐ Talked to audience, not to the equipment
☐ Used facial expressions that supported the message	☐ Used audiovisuals that were attractive and easy to read

I liked the following:

I suggest the following:

Tool 12–1
Review Game

Instructions: Print this page and cut into strips so that you have each statement on a single slip of paper. Ensure that you use only enough for the number of people in the room and that each statement's answer is distributed. If you have an odd number of participants, you will also take a slip so that everyone can participate.

In the ABCs of Presentations, I am the A.

I am accurate.

I am one of the types of presenters we discussed today.

I am enthusiastic.

I am one of the types of presentations we discussed today.

I am persuasive.

In the ABCs of Presentations, I am the B.

I am brief.

I am the percentage of your messages made up of words.

I am 7.

I am a statement that drives you crazy.

I am a red flag.

I am the percentage of your messages determined by tone.

I am 38.

I am a method to overcome nervousness.

I am meditation.

I am how you get to Carnegie Hall.

I am practice, practice, practice.

I am an alternate term for "can't."

I am "can."

In the ABCs of Presentations, I am the C.

I am clear.

Tool 12–2
Presentation Planning Form

Topic:

Date:	Start time and End Time:	Event / Theme:
Attendees:	Location:	Room Setup:

Purpose:

Audience Notes:

Main Points: The concepts I want to get across to my audience are

1.

2.

3.

Opening:

Point One:

S

E

T

Point Two:

S

E

T

continued on next page

Tool 12–2, continued

Presentation Planning Form

Point Three:

S

E

T

Review and Restate:

First Closing:

Question-and-Answer Period:

Second Closing:

Tool 12–3

Pre-Presentation Questionnaire

Instructions: Here are some questions that will help target the presentation to the intended audience. Complete the top portion of the questionnaire and use it to interview those who request a presentation from you. Also, ask to receive any printed background information, such as newsletters, brochures, mission statements, or other materials that will help you learn more about the group attending your presentation.

Topic _____

Presentation Date_____ Start Time_____ End Time_____

Organization Name _____

Contact Name _____ Title_____

Phone _____ Email_____

1. What is the purpose and/or theme of this meeting?_____

_____

2. Is this part of a larger conference or convention?_____

_____

3. If so, what are the dates of the conference?_____

_____

4. How many attendees will be in the audience?_____

_____

5. Audience profile: % female_____ % male _____

_____

6. Average education level_____ Age range _____

_____

7. Dress code_____

_____

continued on next page

Tool 12–3, continued
Pre-Presentation Questionnaire

8. What do I want attendees to know, feel, or learn from my presentation?

9. What is on the program just before my presentation?

10. What is on the program just after my presentation?

11. How will the room be set for my presentation?

12. Here is the list of audiovisual equipment I'll need:

13. Are there any other facts, challenges, or concerns I should know about the group that would help me prepare this presentation?

14. Are there any travel, lodging, parking, or other considerations we need to discuss?

Tool 12–4
Presentation Checklist

Instructions: To ensure that you prepare adequately for a presentation, use the following checklist. Consider when the presentation will take place and date your deadlines backward from that date, being sure to give yourself extra time as a safeguard against unexpected events.

ACTION	DEADLINE
Survey the contact person for expectations.	
Learn about the audience, event, and site.	
Identify the purpose, and write it as a single statement.	
Prioritize the main ideas.	
Develop the introduction.	
Develop first and second closings.	
Research and compile data.	
Draft the presentation.	
Complete a draft of the visual aids.	
Complete the final version of the presentation.	
Complete the final version of the visual aids.	
Create notes for the presentation.	
Practice the presentation.	
Time the presentation.	
Practice for possible questions.	
Rehearse with an audience.	
Practice with the visual aids.	
Hold a dress rehearsal.	
Confirm details with the contact person.	
Deliver the presentation.	

Tool 12–5

On-site Checklist

Instructions: Use this checklist to ensure that you address all elements that will affect your presentation. Create a folder for each presentation you'll deliver, and keep this checklist and other planning forms inside it.

Organization_____

Contact _____   Title _____

Phone _____   Cell _____

Email _____   Fax _____

Facility_____

Contact _____   Title _____

Phone _____   Cell _____

Email _____   Fax _____

Event_____

Day/Date _____   Start Time _____ End Time _____

Location _____   Number of Attendees _____

Notes _____   _____

Room Setup *(circle one)*

auditorium style

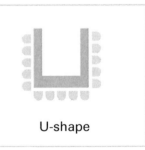

U-shape

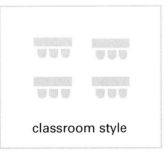

classroom style

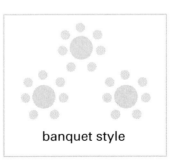

banquet style

continued on next page

Tool 12–5, continued

On-site Checklist

Notes

Audiovisual

☐ CD/cassette player ☐ Easel ☐ Flipchart

☐ Lavaliere microphone ☐ LCD projector ☐ Microphone

☐ Overhead projector ☐ Podium ☐ Projection screen

☐ TV/VCR/DVD player ☐ Other _____

Preparation

☐ Tested equipment

☐ Performed sound check

☐ Checked markers for ink

☐ Checked number of flipchart pages

☐ Checked other audiovisual aids

☐ Know location of registration desk _____

☐ Know name of person who will meet me on-site _____

☐ Know location of light controls _____

☐ Know location of air and heat controls _____

☐ Know name and number to call for heating/cooling issues _____

☐ Know location of restrooms _____

☐ Checked on potentially noisy groups in other rooms

☐ Know where to park _____

☐ Know location of drinks and snacks _____

☐ Know location of spare bulbs, extension cords _____

☐ Know location of copy machine/fax _____

☐ Know guidelines for what can be affixed to the walls _____

☐ Reviewed fire alarm procedures

continued on next page

Tool 12–5, continued

On-site Checklist

Items to Bring

☐ Computer	☐ Lavaliere microphone	☐ Giveaways
☐ LCD projector	☐ Flipchart	☐ Pens/pencils
☐ Overhead projector	☐ Easel	☐ Masking/painter's tape
☐ TV/VCR/DVD player	☐ Markers	☐ Extension cord
☐ Recorder	☐ Notes	☐ Cell phone
☐ Video camera	☐ PowerPoint presentation	☐ Personal toiletries
☐ CD/cassette player	☐ Handouts	☐ Breath mints/spray
☐ Microphone	☐ Resources	
☐ Other_____		

Tool 12–6
Tips for Delivering Presentations

The Best Tips for Vocal Quality

1. Practice varying your inflection by reading passages from children's books because that type of delivery lets you exaggerate and experiment with your vocal tone and range.

2. Before you speak, don't eat heavily or drink soda or milk. Carbonated beverages will give you a dry mouth, and milk products can make you feel like you need to clear your throat.

3. Try deep-breathing exercises before your presentation. Practice using your diaphragm so that your stomach puffs out, but your shoulders don't rise.

4. Practice by recording your speech. Listen to identify what vocal qualities you need to work on.

5. Vary the pitch of your voice. Our voices often go higher when we're nervous, so try breathing exercises to help normalize your voice.

6. Vary your tone, volume, and pace to add emphasis and color to your presentation.

7. Warm up by stretching your face and neck before the presentation.

8. Use practice phrases to help you improve your enunciation.

9. Don't end sentences with an upward tone like you do when you ask a question.

10. Articulate plosives, such as *b, d, t,* and *k,* especially at the end of words. This helps with your diction.

The Best Tips for Using Presentation Notes

1. Do not read your presentation directly from a script. Use notes so you're not tempted to read it word-for-word.

2. Highlight your notes to help you find key passages easily.

3. If using full sheets of paper, don't write on the bottom third of the page. You'll be looking too far down to read it and the audience will be looking at the top of your head.

4. If using note cards, be sure to write large enough to read. Many meeting locations have lower lighting at the podium.

5. Number the pages of your notes. If you drop them, you'll be able to get them back in order more easily.

6. Even if you memorize your presentation, have a set of notes available in case you forget or get nervous.

continued on next page

Tool 12–6, continued

Tips for Delivering Presentations

7. Memorize the opening and closing of your speech. This lets you present those elements with authority and confidence.

8. Write down hints on your notes to remind yourself to pause or slow down.

9. Use your visual aids for notes. The borders of transparencies can be used to write notes. On flipchart pages, you also can write notes in pencil that are invisible to the audience.

10. Rehearse with your notes so that you develop a feel for where the segments are on the pages or cards. This makes it easier to find the information when you glance down at your notes during the presentation.

The Best Phrases to Use When Facilitating

1. *Are we getting off track?* This is a good question to remind people of the focus topic and to bring the conversation back on target.

2. *That's a great question.* This gives you time to think.

3. *I've never had that question before. Let me find out for you.* We should not be afraid to admit that we don't know an answer.

4. *Let's not all talk at once. You first. Then you.* When conversations get out of hand, it's your job as facilitator to make sure everyone plays fair.

5. *Why don't we take a short break?* Sometimes, when tempers flare or it seems that there's no resolution, stepping away and taking a breather is the best solution.

6. *Let's hear from some of the folks who haven't had a chance to give their ideas yet.* When a few people are dominating the conversation, this is a good method to give others a chance to talk.

7. *Could you rephrase that question?* If you can't understand a question, this can be a useful way to get another chance to hear it. If you still don't understand, ask someone else in the audience to restate it for you.

8. *Let's put that one in the parking lot.* When there's a topic that's important, but not on the current agenda it's a good idea to keep a sheet titled "The Parking Lot" to capture those stray ideas or queries for later discussion.

9. *So, what have we decided?* Having the group summarize what action is next is a good way to confirm and remind everyone of the agreed action.

10. *What do you think?* Asking for input from the silent members of the group can solicit some surprisingly good ideas that could have been missed.

Tool 12–7

Top Tips for Presentation Gestures and Body Language

- **Take the body language quiz.** Rate your body language. Is your posture straight? Are your gestures natural and unforced? Are your body movements fluid and comfortable? Does your face display a pleasant expression? Are you making a connection with your eyes? All of these signal confidence and build rapport with your audience.

- **The eyes have it.** Darting eyes make people nervous. Staring at people for too long makes them uncomfortable. How do you decide what's long enough to look at a person? Follow the same rules you do when speaking one-on-one. Three to 5 seconds is fine to look before moving on to the next person. And if you're not comfortable looking your audience directly in the eyes, remember that you can look at foreheads or right over their heads. It gives the same effect as eye contact.

- **Find your friendlies.** We've all noticed that some people have friendly faces. They smile back at you. They nod and respond when you acknowledge them. Find these people in your audience and, when you get nervous or thrown off course, look back at them for reassurance.

- **Use the pause.** This is the best method for looking calm even when you're not. Because of nervousness, many speakers start talking on their way to the podium. Don't fall prey to this urge. Walk to the podium and take a moment to put your notes down. Take a breath, look around at audience members, smile, and silently count to three. Then you can start your presentation. It's a sign of confidence that will earn respect before you even say your first word.

- **Use big moves or not at all.** Keep your hand gestures above the waist. Gestures below the waist look nervous and don't convey confidence. If you don't feel comfortable with gestures, don't use them. Forced gestures look worse than none. (Watch a hometown car commercial and you'll understand what I mean.)

- **Show the audience what you want them to do.** Use prompting gestures to help your audience understand what you want them to do. Raise your hand to show you want them to respond that way. Clap to get them to start applauding. It's part of leading by example.

- **Smile like you just found a quarter.** A smile is the best gesture you can use. It not only makes you feel more confident, but it also helps your audience feel less stressed. After all, they want you to do well. There's nothing more uncomfortable for them than watching a nervous person who looks like he or she wants to cry.

- **Attention, please.** When someone in the audience speaks, use active listening gestures that show you're paying attention. Actions such as maintaining eye contact, nodding, smiling, and moving closer to the speaker assure that person that she or he has your full attention.

- **Shake it off.** Don't worry if you're shaking. The audience can't see it. What feels huge at the podium is not even noticeable at a distance. And those pauses that feel like an hour are usually not more than a few seconds. Keep all of that in mind to maintain perspective.

continued on next page

Tool 12–7, continued

Top Tips for Presentation Gestures and Body Language

◆ **Break the habit.** Eliminate distracting habits. Videotape yourself and watch objectively for actions like rocking, swaying, fidgeting, jingling pocket change, adjusting hair or clothing, or leaning on the podium. Start working to avoid these movements.

◆ **Avoid wardrobe malfunctions.** Don't wear a new outfit. Standing in front of a group is not the time to find out that the shirt won't stay buttoned or that the shoes hurt too much to stand for 20 minutes. Don't wear jewelry that you're tempted to play with. Wear something tried and true.

◆ **Remember that your body talks.** Crossed arms can make people feel like you're closed off. Hands on hips can make it look like you're mad at them. Looking at your watch makes it seem like you're ready to run out the door. Be aware of all of these signals and practice positive body talk.

◆ **Take a walk.** Try stepping out from behind the podium and moving around during your presentation. It not only helps keep the audience's attention, but it lets you work off a little nervous energy.

Tool 12–8

Guidelines for Visual Aids

VISUAL AID	GROUP SIZE	QUICK NOTES
Flipcharts	Small groups	*Pros:* ◆ Are quick to make and inexpensive ◆ Are excellent for small groups and planning sessions ◆ Help the speaker proceed through the material ◆ Provide the audience with something to look at in addition to the speaker ◆ Can be prepared both prior to and during the presentation ◆ Can be used to record audience questions and comments ◆ Can include notes written in pencil as cues for the speaker ◆ Are readily available in most meeting rooms *Cons:* ◆ Require practice to write legibly and quickly ◆ Are not suitable for use in a large audience setting ◆ May be difficult to transport
Handouts	Groups of all sizes	*Pros:* ◆ Are quick to prepare and inexpensive ◆ Are excellent for groups of any size ◆ Enable the audience to focus on the presentation instead of taking notes ◆ Can include space for kinesthetic learners to take notes ◆ Can include any complex visuals that could not be seen clearly on a screen ◆ Ensure that the information is received exactly as the instructor desires *Cons:* ◆ Can distract audience by allowing them to read during the presentation ◆ Can serve as a distraction if handed out during the presentation
Overhead transparencies	Medium to large groups	*Pros:* ◆ Are good for basic charts and information ◆ Can be used for audiences of 20 to 50 people ◆ Can be produced quickly and inexpensively on a copier ◆ Can be used without turning off lights in the room ◆ Can be prepared both prior to and during the presentation

continued on next page

Tool 12–8, continued

Guidelines for Visual Aids

VISUAL AID	GROUP SIZE	QUICK NOTES
PowerPoint presentations	Groups of all sizes	◆ Can include notes written on the cardboard border as cues for the speaker ◆ Are readily available in most meeting rooms *Cons:* ◆ Are sometimes hard to project large enough to be read from the back of the room ◆ Are subject to keystoning (where image does not sit squarely on the screen) ◆ Require the speaker to stay close to the projector to change overheads *Pros:* ◆ Are inexpensive and easily updated ◆ Can easily include attractive designs and clip art ◆ Allow smooth transitions between slides ◆ Can be operated with remote control, enabling the speaker to move around the room ◆ Make it easy to create handouts directly from slides ◆ Deliver a professional image *Cons:* ◆ Can be difficult to restart if the computer malfunctions ◆ Require some software experience in preparing presentations ◆ Can be distracting if too many effects are used
Projection boards	Small to medium groups	*Pros:* ◆ Are versatile and can be used with computers, video, and CD-ROM ◆ Can be used to take notes and email to the group ◆ Permit quick changes during the presentation ◆ Can include professional graphics and designs ◆ Can be used for Webinars and for teaching computer programs *Cons:* ◆ Require a backup plan in case of technical failures ◆ Require expensive replacement bulbs ◆ Require a large screen ◆ Can be difficult to set up

Tool 12–9

Flipchart Tips

Tips for Writing on a Flipchart

◆ Print legibly.

◆ Don't print in all caps. It's harder to read.

◆ Make letters 1–2 inches tall so the audience can read them. Use the pages with grid lines on them if you need help in sizing and printing in a straight line.

◆ Use dark colors for writing and lighter colors for highlighting.

◆ Use bullets to make points stand out.

◆ Make light notes in pencil on the side of flipchart pages for your own cheat sheets (the audience can't see these).

◆ When noting audience responses, print their exact words unless you get permission to paraphrase.

◆ Use extra colors to keep it interesting, but don't print text in more than three colors on one page.

◆ Use key words and phrases rather than long sentences.

◆ Practice drawing a few cartoon faces or icons for fun emphasis of points. You can even pencil these in ahead of time.

◆ Rule of Sevens: No more than seven lines of text per page; no more than seven words per line.

Tips for Using a Flipchart while Speaking

◆ Stand to the side as you write or speak.

◆ Never talk to your chart. Touch, turn, and tell.

◆ If you have a lot of information, prepare flipcharts ahead of time.

◆ If you have prepared flipchart pages in advance, leave two blank pages between them so your audience doesn't see through to the next page.

continued on next page

Tool 12-9, continued

Flipchart Tips

- ◆ If you plan to refer to the pages later, tape them up on the walls.

- ◆ Keep pre-torn pieces of masking or printer's tape on the back of your easel for quick posting of pages.

- ◆ Use tape tabs to mark the pages for easy page turning.

- ◆ Turn pages in one motion to keep them from creasing at the top.

- ◆ Tear with confidence. Tear pages in one motion and they'll come off more cleanly than if you try to tear a little at a time.

To Use or Not to Use

- ◆ Don't use flipcharts for large audiences. They're too hard to see. Test by sitting in the back row to see if you can read the page.

- ◆ You can solicit a volunteer to be your scribe and keep notes if you want to move around during the discussion.

- ◆ If your handwriting is illegible, use a scribe at all times or don't use flipcharts.

Tool 12–10

Developing Your Sense of Humor

Add new endings to old clichés:

- A bird in hand . . .

- My cup runneth over . . .

- If at first you don't succeed . . .

Play Good News, Bad News:

- The bad news is you're fired; the good news is . . .

- The bad news is the local team lost; the good news is . . .

Read the Headlines:

- Apathy Study Needs Participants

- Three States Hit by Blizzard; One Is Missing

- Lawyer to Offer Poor Free Advice

Watch for Bumper Stickers:

- I still miss my ex-husband, but my aim is getting better.

- As long as there are tests, there will be prayer in school.

- Lightning never strikes twice, but isn't once enough?

Check Out Quotes That Strike Your Funny Bone

- A verbal contract isn't worth the paper it's written on. *–Samuel Goldwyn*

- Baseball is 90 percent mental. The other half is physical. *–Yogi Berra*

- Seize the Day. Remember those women on the Titanic who waved off the dessert cart. *–Erma Bombeck*

Tool 12–11
Icebreaker and Energizer Activities

The Bouncing Ball Introductions

Grab a beach ball and form a circle. Toss the ball to some person across the circle. That person introduces himself or herself, then throws the ball across the circle to another person. Everyone continues to throw the ball around in the same order and they have to call the next person's name before they throw it to him or her.

Team Competition

Have teams create lists of questions and answers. Then have them compete against each other. It's a fun way to review—without calling it a review.

Call to Order

Instead of calling for order, try a harmonica, a bell, or even singing. Yes, they'll think you're going crazy . . . and they'll get quiet to watch it happen!

Post-Lunch Wake-Ups

Schedule an afternoon energy break. Try 5 minutes of aerobics, a lively exercise, or save dessert for an afternoon snack.

True or False

Ask each person in the groups to list on paper four facts about themselves. Three should be true and one should be false. They read these lists aloud to the other members of their group and those members try to guess which is false. The person tells the correct answer.

Speed Meeting

Ask people to circulate and speak to one person at a time to get acquainted. After 1 minute, call "Change" and have everyone move to meet a new person. Do this until they've had the opportunity to meet a number of people in the group.

Improv Questions

Create some scenes for participants to act out, such as meeting the world's toughest customer. Have volunteer teams come forward. They will act out the scene, but they can only talk in questions. As soon as they speak in something other than a question, a teammate takes over. See who can last the longest without getting tossed out.

Improv Characters

Everyone gets a card with a character trait listed on it. At their tables, they carry on a discussion as if they had this trait, but they can't tell what it is. At the end of the time limit, everyone tries to guess the character traits at their tables. Vote on best actor for a prize.

continued on next page

Tool 12–11, continued

Icebreaker and Energizer Activities

Card Greetings

Pass out an index card to each attendee. Have each person write three statements about themselves on the card. Collect the cards, shuffle them, and pass them out so everyone has someone else's card. Ask attendees to find the person whose card they have and to introduce themselves.

A Penny for Your Thoughts

Gather people into small groups and give each person a penny. Ask everyone to introduce themselves to the group and to talk about what they were doing during the year the coin was minted.

Candy Breaks

Have a basket of brand-name candies, such as Snickers, M&Ms, and Almond Joy bars. Ask each person to pick a candy. Then tell them that, based on the candy each chose, they must share an experience with the class. For example, if someone has selected a Snickers bar, she or he must tell about a funny incident. Someone who has picked M&Ms must tell something they normally keep mum about. An Almond Joy picker has to tell what makes him or her joyful. Make up your own list of candy requirements.

Favorites

Have each person list her or his favorite TV show, movie, hobby, color, and animal on a card and hand them in to you. Read these aloud and ask the group to guess which person's card you're reading.

The Name Game

To each attendee's back, attach a card with a famous person's name written on it. Each person's task is to figure out whose name he or she is wearing. People may ask only yes/no questions. If they get a "yes" answer, they can continue to ask questions of the same person. As soon as they get a "no" answer, they have to move on to question someone else. Each person announces her or his guesses at the end of 15 minutes.

Training Instrument 12–1

Introductions

Instructions: In the top spaces on this sheet, write your notes about the person you're going to introduce. In the additional rows, write the names of your classmates and some interesting facts about each of them.

NAMES	INTERESTING FACTS
Your interviewee:	

Training Instrument 12–2
Red Flags

Instructions: The left column is for red flag statements. The right column is for statements that could be used to replace those red flags.

RED FLAG	ALTERNATIVE STATEMENT
Example: We've always done it that way.	
Example: That won't work.	
Example: But...	

Training Instrument 12–3

Tone

     Instructions: Your practice phrase should be a phrase you use often at work. List emotions that people experience in the workplace.

MY PRACTICE PHRASE	EMOTIONS

Reminder:

Training Instrument 12–4
Body Language

Instructions: Every day we send messages without even saying a word. List some examples of body language and write a word or phrase to describe how you interpret each of those actions.

BODY LANGUAGE	INTERPRETATIONS
Example: Stroking chin	Thoughtful

Reminder:

Training Instrument 12–5

Overcoming Nervousness

Instructions: Use the rows below to list and rank your group's ideas to help overcome the nervousness of delivering a presentation. As the entire class discusses this, add any additional ideas from the other groups' lists that you feel might be useful to you.

RANK	IDEAS

Training Instrument 12–6
Guidelines for Preparing a Presentation Planning Form

Instructions: While listening to the instructor explain the portions of the following form, make notes in the sections below to help you complete such a form (Tool 12–2) for each presentation you plan.

PRESENTATION PLANNING FORM

Topic:

Date:	Start time and End Time:	Event / Theme:
Attendees:	Location:	Room Setup:

Purpose:

Audiencè Notes:

Main Points: The concepts I want to get across to my audience are

1.

2.

3.

Opening:

Point One:

S

E

T

continued on next page

Training Instrument 12–6, continued

Guidelines for Preparing a Presentation Planning Form

Point Two:

S

E

T

Point Three:

S

E

T

Review and Restate:

First Closing:

Question-and-Answer Period:

Second Closing:

Training Instrument 12–7

Brainstorming

Instructions:

1. Write your main topic in the center of the circle.

2. Moving outward from the circle, begin writing any words or phrases that come to mind about the topic. **Don't edit, judge, or censor any ideas.**

3. As you fill up one area of the block, move to another area and continue the process.

4. When you've filled the block and exhausted all your ideas, survey the page.

5. Find terms that seem related and circle them. As you begin to define concepts, either circle the related words/phrases in the same colors or draw different kinds of lines to connect the words/phrases (for example, dotted, thick, thin, and zigzag lines).

6. When you've grouped all the words/phrases, you have the main divisions of your presentation.

Training Instrument 12–8

The S-E-T Formula

QUESTIONS *(choose one and circle it):*

1. Is your job difficult?

2. Why should we read your favorite book?

3. Why should we see your favorite movie?

4. What is your favorite vacation spot?

5. Why should we vote for you for president?

Using the S-E-T Formula

Instructions: Use this column to make notes and brainstorm on the steps of S-E-T. Answer the questions and follow the instructions in each section.	*Instructions: Use this column to prepare the final wording of your S-E-T answer.*
What is the basic answer to the question?	Short answer:
What are three points that support the basic answer?	Evidence:
Summarize how the evidence supports your answer, and decide what statement you'll use to move the conversation back to the other person.	Transition:

Training Instrument 12–9

S-E-T Practice

QUESTIONS *(choose one and circle it):*

1. Why do you think body language is important?

2. Do you think tone is important in presentations?

3. What do you think is the worst Red Flag statement?

4. What is your favorite idea for overcoming nervousness?

5. Why does everyone need to take a class on presentation skills?

Using the S-E-T Formula

Instructions: Use this column to make notes and brainstorm on the steps of S-E-T. Answer the questions and follow the instructions in each section.	*Instructions: Use this column to prepare the final wording of your S-E-T answer.*
What is the basic answer to the question?	Short answer:
What are three points that support the basic answer?	Evidence:
Summarize how the evidence supports your answer, and decide what statement you'll use to move the conversation back to the other person.	Transition:

Training Instrument 12–10

Presentation Action Plan

Instructions: This form is for you to use in brainstorming about the topic for your presentation at the conclusion of this workshop.

PRESENTATION TOPIC IDEAS

Informational/Instructional

1. Teach us how to do something.

2. Teach us one of the topics from this workshop.

3.

4.

Inspirational

1. Tell us a story of some event that changed your life.

2. Tell us an anecdote you've heard and what point it proves.

3.

4.

Persuasive

1. Pick some item in the room and try to sell it to us.

2. Persuade us to take a class on presentation skills.

3.

4.

Training Instrument 12–11
Building Rapport

Instructions: In the first column, list things that your group members may have in common. In the second column, write the specific shared items relating to each topic.

POSSIBLE COMMONALITIES	ALL MEMBERS OF OUR GROUP
Example: Pets	Everyone has a dog
Example: Hobbies	

Training Instrument 12–12

Microsoft PowerPoint Guidelines

- ♦ Don't type your presentation word-for-word on the slides.

- ♦ Use color and designs to add interest.

- ♦ Don't read your presentation from the slides.

- ♦ Don't overdo the special effects.

- ♦ Use a consistent design.

- ♦ Use consistent graphics that are similar in appearance.

- ♦ Include only essential information.

- ♦ Use contrasting colors.

- ♦ Use the Rule of Sevens: no more than seven lines per slide, and no more than seven words per line.

- ♦ Use only one idea per slide.

- ♦ Use simple font styles for readability.

- ♦ Don't use more than two fonts per slide.

- ♦ Don't use all CAPS.

- ♦ Use fonts in sizes ranging from 18 to 48 points.

- ♦ Follow bullets with a capital letter.

- ♦ Make graphics face the middle of the slide.

- ♦ Use no more than three graphics per slide.

- ♦ Proofread carefully.

- ♦ Formulate a backup plan in case of equipment failure.

continued on next page

Training Instrument 12–12, continued
Microsoft PowerPoint Guidelines

What's Wrong With This Picture?

Instructions: Review the PowerPoint guidelines and, on the lines below, list all the problems you can find on this slide.

Training Instrument 12–13

Challenging Situations

Instructions: Listed below are some key phrases and ideas for handling challenging situations while delivering a presentation. Can you think of others?

CHALLENGING SITUATION	POSSIBLE SOLUTIONS
Talkers	◆ Stand near the disruptive parties. ◆ Ask for their comments. ◆ Ask them to refrain from talking. ◆ If the behavior persists, take a break and take the parties aside to discuss the problem.
Disagreement	Try these phrases: ◆ Let's be fair. ◆ Interesting thought. ◆ Could we put that on the back burner for now?
Ringing cell phone	◆ Gently remind the group of the no-cell-phone ground rule.
Two or more people talking at one time	Try these phrases: ◆ You first, then you. ◆ Are we getting off track?
Confusing question from an audience member	Try these phrases: ◆ Could you break that question down a little further for me? ◆ So what you're saying is . . . . ◆ Does someone else have an insight on this statement?
One person who won't stop talking.	Try these phrases: ◆ How about if we get some ideas from this (the other) side of the room? ◆ Let's get someone else to help us out on this one.

Training Instrument 12–13, continued
Challenging Situations

Instructions: Copy this page and cut into strips. Place the strips in a box or other container for attendees to draw from. Each attendee will give ideas on how she or he could handle the situation described on the strip of paper drawn from the box. Invite others to join in with their ideas, and be ready to add some ideas of your own.

Your Disruptive Behavior: An audience member interrupts you for help with a crossword puzzle. What do you do?

Your Disruptive Behavior: A woman in the front row is talking to someone on her cell phone. What do you do?

Your Disruptive Behavior: Two people start talking in the front row. What do you do?

Your Disruptive Behavior: Someone asks a really dumb question that has nothing to do with the subject! What do you say?

Your Disruptive Behavior: A man in the audience falls asleep and starts snoring loudly. What do you do?

Your Disruptive Behavior: Someone in the audience starts arguing with one of the points in your presentation and won't stop talking. What do you do?

Your Disruptive Behavior: A person in the group just can't seem to comprehend what you're talking about. What do you do?

Your Disruptive Behavior: Someone starts trying to talk you into stopping your presentation for a break right now. The last break was less than 30 minutes ago. What do you do?

Your Disruptive Behavior: You have a know-it-all in your audience who won't stop talking. What do you do?

Your Disruptive Behavior: Someone in your audience is having a sneezing attack. What do you do?

Your Disruptive Behavior: Someone in the audience obviously had too many martinis for lunch. What do you do?

Training Instrument 12–14

Practice Session Planning Form

Instructions: Select one of the presentation ideas from Training Instrument 12–10. Then use this Practice Session Planning Form to design your talk.

PRESENTATION PLANNING FORM

Topic:

Introduction:

Point One:

S

E

T

continued on next page

Training Instrument 12–14, continued
Practice Session Planning Form

Point Two:

S

E

T

Point Three:

S

E

T

Review and Closing:

Training Instrument 12–15

Continued Development Action Plan

Instructions: Are you committed to continuing to develop the skills you've practiced in this workshop? Demonstrate your commitment by signing this statement. Then address your envelope so that your workshop buddy can mail this reminder to you in 30 days.

I, _____ , am serious about developing my presentation skills.

These are the items I committed to doing after the workshop:

◆ Teach one process from this class within 24 hours.

◆ Prepare an elevator speech within 7 days.

◆ Commit to one presentation within 1 month.

If I have done these things, this letter is to congratulate me. If I have not done them, this is a friendly reminder that the time to practice presentation skills is right now!

The box below is for my workshop buddy to write a joke, a story, an anecdote, or some other bonus item that I can add to my file of great openings and closings.

This bonus item is from _____

Training Instrument 12–16

Practice Session

Instructions: Use this form to make notes and brainstorm on the steps of Short Answer – Evidence – Transition.

Using the S-E-T Formula

Instructions: Use this column to make notes and brainstorm on the steps of S-E-T. Answer the questions and follow the instructions in each section.	*Instructions:* Use this column to prepare the final wording of your S-E-T answer.
What is the basic answer to the question?	Short answer:
What are three points that support the basic answer?	Evidence:
Summarize how the evidence supports your answer, and decide what statement you'll use to move the conversation back to the other person.	Transition:

◆

Using the Website

Access the website www.astd.org/PresentationSkillsTraining.

DOWNLOADS

Contents of the Website

The website that accompanies this presentation skills training workbook contains three types of files. All of the files can be used on a variety of computer platforms.

- **Adobe .pdf documents.** These include assessments, tools, and training instruments.

- **Microsoft PowerPoint presentations.** The website includes separate presentations for the one-hour, half-day, one-day, and two-day workshops.

- **Microsoft PowerPoint files for overhead transparency masters.** These files have been formatted to make them more suited for use on overhead projectors. They make it easy to print viewgraphs and handouts in black-and-white.

Computer Requirements

To read or print the .pdf files on the website, you must have Adobe Acrobat Reader software installed on your system. The program can be downloaded free of charge from the Adobe Website, *www.adobe.com*.

To use or make changes to the contents of the PowerPoint presentation files on the website, you must have Microsoft PowerPoint software installed on your system. If you simply want to view the PowerPoint documents, you must have an appropriate viewer installed on your computer. Microsoft provides various viewers free for downloading from its Website, *www.microsoft.com*.

Printing from the Website

TEXT FILES

You can print the training materials using Adobe Acrobat Reader. Simply open the .pdf file and print as many copies as you need. The following .pdf documents can be printed directly from the website.

- ◆ Assessment 12–1: Self-Assessment

- ◆ Assessment 12–2: Program Evaluation

- ◆ Assessment 12–3: Learning Styles

- ◆ Assessment 12–4: Presenter Evaluation

- ◆ Tool 12–1: Review Game

- ◆ Tool 12–2: Presentation Planning Form

- ◆ Tool 12–3: Pre-Presentation Questionnaire

- ◆ Tool 12–4: Presentation Checklist

- ◆ Tool 12–5: On-site Checklist

- ◆ Tool 12–6: Tips for Delivering Presentations

- ◆ Tool 12–7: Top Tips for Presentation Gestures and Body Language

- ◆ Tool 12–8: Guidelines for Visual Aids

- ◆ Tool 12–9: Flipchart Tips

- ◆ Tool 12–10: Developing Your Sense of Humor

- ◆ Tool 12–11: Icebreaker and Energizer Activities

- ◆ Training Instrument 12–1: Introductions

- ◆ Training Instrument 12–2: Red Flags

- ◆ Training Instrument 12–3: Tone

- ◆ Training Instrument 12–4: Body Language

- ◆ Training Instrument 12–5: Overcoming Nervousness

- ◆ Training Instrument 12–6: Guidelines for Preparing a Presentation Planning Form

- ◆ Training Instrument 12–7: Brainstorming

- ◆ Training Instrument 12–8: The S-E-T Formula

- ◆ Training Instrument 12–9: S-E-T Practice

- ◆ Training Instrument 12–10: Presentation Action Plan

- ◆ Training Instrument 12–11: Building Rapport

- ◆ Training Instrument 12–12: Microsoft PowerPoint Guidelines

- ◆ Training Instrument 12–13: Challenging Situations

- ◆ Training Instrument 12–14: Practice Session Planning Form

- ◆ Training Instrument 12–15: Continued Development Action Plan

- ◆ Training Instrument 12–16: Practice Session

POWERPOINT SLIDES

You can print the presentation slides directly from the website using Microsoft PowerPoint. Simply open the .ppt files and print as many copies as you need. You also can make handouts of the presentations by printing three slides per page. These slides will be in color, with design elements embedded. Power-Point also permits you to print these in grayscale or black-and-white, although printing from the overhead masters file will yield better black-and-white representations. Many trainers who use laptop computers to project their presentations bring along viewgraphs just in case there are glitches in the system. The overhead masters can be printed from the PowerPoint .pps files.

Adapting the PowerPoint Slides

You can modify or otherwise customize the slides by opening and editing them in the appropriate application. However, you must credit the original source of the material—it is illegal to pass it off as your own work. You may indicate that a document was adapted from this workbook, written by Christee Atwood and copyrighted by ASTD. The files will open as "Read Only," so you will need to save them onto your hard drive under a different file name before you adapt them.

Table A–1

Navigating Through a PowerPoint Presentation

KEY	POWERPOINT "SHOW" ACTION
Space bar *or* Enter *or* Mouse click	Advance through custom animations embedded in the presentation
Backspace	Back up to the last projected element of the presentation
Escape	Abort the presentation
B *or* b B *or* b *(repeat)*	Blank the screen to black Resume the presentation
W *or* w W *or* w *(repeat)*	Blank the screen to white Resume the presentation

Showing the PowerPoint Presentations

On the website, the following PowerPoint presentations are included:

- ◆ *One-Hour.ppt*

- ◆ *Half-Day.ppt*

- ◆ *One-Day.ppt*

- ◆ *Two-Day.ppt*

Having the presentations in a .ppt format means that they automatically show full-screen when you double-click a file name. You also can open Microsoft PowerPoint and launch the presentations from there.

Use the space bar, the enter key, or mouse clicks to advance through a show. Press the backspace key to back up. Use the escape key to abort a presentation. If you want to blank the screen to black while the group discusses a point, press the B key. Pressing it again restores the show. If you want to blank the screen to a white background, do the same with the W key.

I strongly recommend that trainers practice making presentations with the PowerPoint slides before using them in live training situations. You should be confident that you can cogently expand on the points featured in the presentations and discuss the methods for working through them. If you want to engage your training participants fully (rather than worrying about how to show the next slide), become familiar with this simple technology before you need to use it. A good practice is to insert notes into the Speaker's Notes feature of the PowerPoint program, print them out, and have them in front of you when you present the slides.

For Further Reading

Alessandra, Tony, and Phil Hunsaker. 1993. *Communicating at Work*. New York: Fireside Books.

Booher, Dianna. 2003. *Speak with Confidence*. New York: McGraw-Hill.

Burrows, Terry. 2000. *Creating Presentations*. New York: Dorling Kindersley.

Daley, Kevin. 2004. *Talk Your Way to the Top*. New York: McGraw-Hill.

Hindle, Tim. 1998. *Making Presentations*. New York: Dorling Kindersley Publishing.

Holliday, Micki. 2000. *Secrets of Power Presentations*. Franklin Lakes, NJ: Career Press.

Jacobi, Jeffrey. 1996. *The Vocal Advantage*. Paramus, NJ: Prentice Hall.

Jeary, Tony. 2004. *Life Is a Series of Presentations*. New York: Fireside Books.

Jolles, Robert L. 1993. *How to Run Seminars and Workshops*. New York: John Wiley & Sons.

Negino, Tom. 2005. *Creating a Presentation in PowerPoint*. Berkeley, CA: Peachpit Press.

Nelson, Robert B., and Jennifer Wallick. 1990. *Making Effective Presentations*. Glenview, IL: Scott, Foresman.

Orey, Maureen, and Jenni Prisk. 2004. *Communications Skills Training*. Alexandria, VA: ASTD Press.

Peoples, David A. 1992. *Presentations Plus*, 2nd edition. New York: John Wiley & Sons.

Rotondo, Jennifer, and Mike Rotondo, Jr. 2002. *Presentation Skills for Managers*. New York: McGraw-Hill.

Templeton, Melody. 1999. *Schaum's Quick Guide to Great Presentations*. New York: McGraw-Hill.

Christee Gabour Atwood is a speaker, trainer, and knowledge management adviser who specializes in helping companies share the knowledge in their organizations. She has worked with corporations, associations, *Fortune* 500 companies, and governmental entities in analyzing, developing, and presenting programs to develop communication and leadership skills.

Recipient of the 2006 Outstanding Adjunct Faculty Award at Baton Rouge Community College, Atwood's background includes radio personality, television host and anchor, and newspaper and magazine columnist. She also has served as executive director for state associations, editor/publisher of various trade and professional magazines, and CEO of The Communications Workshop, Inc.

Atwood is a master facilitator for the Small Business Training Center in Baton Rouge, Louisiana, and has received training certifications from various organizations, including Franklin Covey and AchieveGlobal. And, because she believes humor is a vital part of effective communications, she also teaches "But UnSeriously Folks!"—a course on the effective use of humor in the workplace, which is based on her experiences in stand-up comedy.

Her other books include *Succession Planning Basics* (ASTD Press 2007) and *Three Feet Under: Journal of a Midlife Crisis,* which is a humorous look at the episodes of midlife. Scheduled for release in 2008 is Atwood's third book with ASTD Press: *Manager Skills Training.* She can be reached at Christee@Christee.biz.

◆

A

action plans
    for half-day program, 47
    learning activities on, 142
    for one-day program, 68
    for one-hour program, 35–36
    training instruments for, 180,
        188
    for two-day program, 94–95, 100
activities, 24
agendas, 3–4, 33–36, 41–47, 56–
        68, 79–101
aggressive behavior, 10, 24, 67, 98
anxiety techniques, 9, 59–62,
        86–88
assessments
    analysis of, 16
    challenges of, 13–14
    of learning styles, 147–48
    of needs, 3
    of participants, 28
    of presenters, 149
    of programs, 146
    of self, 33–34, 42, 57, 80–81,
        145
    tools for, 14–16
attention span, 7
audience, 7, 10, 65–66, 91, 96–97

B

best practices, 23–25
body language, 84–86, 119–20,
        161–62, 173
brainstorming, 91, 124–25, 177

C

CD, 4, 32, 41, 55, 78
challenging situations. *See* disrup-
        tions
checklists, presentation prepara-
        tion, 155–58
communication
    body language as, 84–86, 119–
        20, 161–62, 173
    elevator speeches, 9, 35, 44–45,
        62–63, 94
    gestures as, 96
    impromptu speeches, 99–100,
        168–69

    tone as, 84–85, 117–18, 172
    with words, 84–85, 115–16,
        171
    of workshops, 19–20
continued development, 100

D

discussions, as evaluations, 28
disruptions
    learning activities on, 137
    management of, 10, 24, 67, 98
    training instruments for,
        184–85

E

elevator speeches, 9, 35, 44–45,
        62–63, 94
evaluations
    benefits of, 27
    for half-day program, 47
    methods for, 3, 27–30
    for one-day program, 68
    for one-hour program, 36
    of presenters, 149
    of programs, 146
    for two-day program, 95, 100

F

facilitation, 21, 23–25
flipcharts, 97, 165–66

G

games, 123, 150
gestures, 96
    See also body language
Get Ready, Get SET, Go formula,
        9, 45, 64, 88–89
goals, 17–18, 19, 57, 80
ground rules, 23, 33, 41–42, 56,
        79–80

H

humor, 10, 23, 98, 167

I

icebreakers, 99–100, 168–69
icons, 4–5
impromptu speeches, 34–35,
        43–44, 62, 93

    interviews, as assessments, 15
introductions, 113–14, 170

L

learning activities
    on actions plans, 142
    for brainstorming, 124–25
    on challenging situations,
        115–16, 137
    on communication, 115–20
    on introductions, 113–14
    on nervousness, 121–22
    on PowerPoint, 136
    on presentations, 131–33,
        138–39
    on rapport, 129–30
    review game, 123
    on S-E-T Formula, 126–28
    on speaking opportunities,
        140–41
    on visual aids, 134–35
learning environment, 18–19
learning styles, 10, 24, 97, 147–48
lectures, 23

M

materials
    for half-day program, 39–40
    for one-day program, 53–55
    for one-hour program, 31–32
    for participants, 22–23
    for presenters, 2
    for two-day program, 76–78
messages, parts of, 84–86
methods, of evaluation, 3, 27–29
Microsoft PowerPoint, 97, 136,
        182–83

N

needs assessments, 3
nervousness, 9, 59–62, 86–88,
        121–22, 174

O

objectives, 17–18, 31, 39, 53, 75
observations, as assessments,
        14–15

P

parking lot, 24–25
participants, 22–23, 28, 57, 80
planning
  for presentations, 9, 45–46,
    64–66, 89–91
  tools for, 151–54
  training instruments for,
    186–87
PowerPoint, 97, 136, 182–83
preparation
  for half-day program, 41, 48
  for one-day program, 55–56,
    69
  for one-hour program, 32–33,
    36
  training instruments for, 175–76
  for two-day program, 79
  for workshops, 2, 4, 21–22
presentations
  ABCs, 83–84
  concepts of, 7–11
  delivery of, 96, 159–60
  learning activities on, 131–33,
    138–39
  location of, 156–58
  parts of, 46–47, 66–67, 91–93
  planning for, 9, 45–46, 64–66,
    89–91, 151–54
  preparation for, 9–10, 155–58
  skills for, ix, 3
  tools for, 151–60
  training instruments for, 175–
    76, 186–87
  types of, 1, 8, 42–43, 58–59,
    82–83
  writing, 96
presenters
  evaluation of, 149
  materials for, 2
  types of, 8, 34, 57–58, 81–82
program (half-day)
  action plan, 47
  agenda, 41–47
  CD use, 41
  elevator speeches, 44–45
  evaluation, 47
  ground rules, 41–42
  impromptu speeches, 43–44
  materials, 39–40
  objectives, 39
  preparation for, 41, 48
  presentation types, 42–43
  purpose, 39
  self-assessments, 42
  slides, 49–51
  visual aids, 47

program (one-day)
  action plan, 68
  agenda, 56–68
  CD use, 55
  distractions, 67
  elevator speeches, 62–63
  evaluation, 68
  ground rules, 56
  impromptu speeches, 62
  materials, 53–55
  nervousness, 59–62
  objectives, 53
  preparation for, 55–56, 69
  presentation types, 58–59
  presenter types, 57–58
  purpose, 53
  self-assessments, 57
  slides, 70–73
  visual aids, 67
program (one-hour)
  action plan, 35–36
  agenda, 33–36
  CD use, 32
  elevator speeches, 35
  evaluation, 36
  ground rules, 33
  impromptu speeches, 34–35
  materials, 31–32
  objectives, 31
  preparation for, 32–33, 36
  presenter types, 34
  purpose, 31
  self-assessments, 33–34
  slides, 37–38
program (two-day)
  action plan, 94–95, 100
  agenda, 79–101
  audience, 96–97
  brainstorming, 91
  CD use, 78
  disruptions, 98
  elevator speeches, 94
  evaluation, 95, 100
  gestures, 96
  ground rules, 79–80
  humor, 98
  icebreakers, 99–100
  impromptu speeches, 93
  learning styles, 97
  materials, 76–78
  message parts, 84–86
  nervousness, 86–88
  objectives, 75
  preparation for, 79, 101
  presentation ABCs, 83–84
  presentation types, 82–83
  presenter types, 81–82

purpose, 75
Q&A sessions, 98–99
rapport, 95–96
self-assessments, 80–81
slides, 102–9
visual aids, 97
promotional plan, 19–20

Q

Q&A sessions, 98–99

R

rapport, 9, 95–96, 129–30, 181
records, as assessments, 14
red flags, 115–16, 171
reinforcement, 23
requests, as assessments, 15–16
resources, 2
reviews, 123, 150

S

seating arrangements, 18, 89–90
self-assessments
  assessments for, 145
  as evaluations, 28
  for half-day program, 42
  for one-day program, 57
  for one-hour program, 33–34
  for two-day program, 80–81
S-E-T Formula
  learning activities on, 126–28
  for speeches, 34–35, 43–45,
    62–63, 93–94
  training instruments for, 178–
    79, 189
speaking opportunities, 140–41
speeches, 34–35, 43–45, 62–63,
    93–94
surveys, as assessments, 15

T

techniques, nervousness, 9, 59–
    62, 86–88
tests, as assessments, 14
time, best practices for, 25
tone, 84–85, 117–18, 172
tools
  for assessments, 14–16
  for communication, 161–62
  for flipcharts, 165–66
  for humor, 167
  for icebreakers, 168–69
  presentation checklist, 155
  for presentations, 151–54,
    156–60
  for review game, 150
  for visual aids, 163–66

training instruments
    for action plans, 180, 188
    for brainstorming, 177
    for challenging situations, 171,
        184–85
    for communication, 172–73
    for introductions, 170
    for nervousness, 174
    for PowerPoint, 182–83
    for presentations, 175–76,
        186–87
    for rapport, 181
    for S-E-T Formula, 178–79,
        189

V
visual aids
    abuse of, 10
    for half-day program, 47
    learning activities on, 134–35
    for one-day program, 67
    tools for, 163–66
    for two-day program, 97

W
words, 84–85, 115–16, 171
workbook, 2, 3–4
workshops
    advertisement for, 19–20
    assessments for, 146

    benefits of, ix–x
    best practices, 23–25
    goals for, 17–18, 19
    learning environment, 18–19
    preparation for, 2, 4, 21–22